BAKE HAPPY

Recipes and reflections for a sweet life

*For my mother, Catherine Ritchie Bussi,
with love and thanks always*

BAKE HAPPY

Recipes and reflections for a sweet life

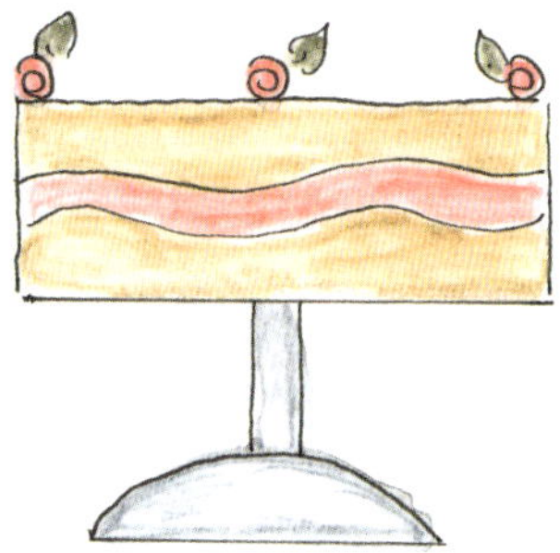

Written and illustrated
by Gail Bussi

Acknowledgements

To all those who have contributed to the book in various ways

Published in 2013 by Struik Lifestyle
(an imprint of Random House Struik (Pty) Ltd))
Company Reg. No. 1966/003153/07
Wembley Square, Solan Road, Cape Town 8001, South Africa
PO Box 1144, Cape Town 8000
www.randomstruik.co.za

Publisher: Linda de Villiers
Design manager: Beverley Dodd
Editor: Cecilia Barfield
Designer: Helen Henn
Illustrator: Gail Bussi
Proofreader and indexer: Anja Grobler

Reproduction: Hirt & Carter Cape (Pty) Ltd
Printing and binding: Toppan Leefung Packaging and Printing Co., Ltd, China

ISBN 978-1-43230-168-2

Contents

Introduction

I have two clear memories of things I loved doing when I was a little girl – reading and baking. (Actually, the baking came first, before I even learned to read.) I think most bakers would agree that they started in the kitchen, standing alongside a mom or dad or granny or aunt, watching as he or she stirred, mixed and added all sorts of ingredients to create a wonderful sort of alchemy in the oven.

Wherever I was in the house, I was drawn to the kitchen like a magnet when I knew my mom was making a cake, or cookies, or scones. She always left a little of the mixture in the bowl for me to scrape up with a spatula. I used to wonder why cake batter or cookie dough sometimes tastes even better before it's baked.

And later, when I was about eight or nine years of age, I was allowed to bake a cake – on my own! – for the very first time. My mom showed quite a lot of faith in me by going out and leaving me to it – only to be greeted by a very sad face when she returned. I couldn't find the vanilla essence, and was convinced that the cake would be a flop without it! Then there was the time I knocked an entire bottle of pink colouring into a bowl of icing – needless to say that was a very colourful cake!

As I say elsewhere in this book, the baking I remember (and which I still do most of the time) was not fancy or time consuming. It was the simple, honest taste of plain cakes and cookies and buttery scones. To this day I have no great love for those towering, gungy cakes, filled with cream, that one often sees in bakeries or restaurants. They might look grand, but the taste is often something of a let down.

From my early baking beginnings I progressed to experimenting with recipes from all over the world, some from cookbooks, others given to me by friends. That's really one of the things I love most about baking, and cooking in general – the sense that one is part of the greater whole, learning something fresh and delicious with each new recipe one tries. It's the sense of continuity and community that I enjoy. So many of the recipes in this book have a history, and when I make them, I am transported to other places and times.

Today there's a big trend towards simpler and less rushed living, which is one I am heartily in favour of – and I think baking can be a big part of that. It's actually difficult to be angry or stressed when one is quietly pottering in the kitchen, rolling out dough or whipping sugar and butter to a light cream. So, apart from having something delicious to eat and share, one is left feeling a lot calmer and more serene.

It is my hope that some of the recipes in this book will become your favourites too, and that you will discover simple joy and tranquillity while practising this kitchen art. That, after all, is what it's all about – a celebration of food, family, friends, laughter and love.

There is a difference between living and just surviving. Find something that you love, and find someone to love ... it's that simple. And that hard.

JOHN CONNOLLY

Sharing Kitchen Warmth

In the childhood memories of every good cook, there's a large kitchen, a warm stove, a simmering pot and a mom.

BARBARA COSTIKYAN

Any book about food and cooking is always about so much more – fundamentally about how the simple kitchen arts are tied together with strings of memory, family, friendship and love, and things that are part of our universal experience. I have had many blessings in my life, but one of the earliest, and best, was that I grew up in a nurturing home, with a mom who had lots of time, patience and love. That warmth was most evident in the kitchen, which was always the 'heart of our home', and from where a seemingly endless stream of simple yet delicious meals and baked goods would appear to delight both family and friends.

And, of course, there were other kitchens; those of my aunts and neighbours and my mother's friends – all a part of the kitchen warmth I knew and treasured. So, the recipes in this section – and indeed throughout the book – have their origin in many different kitchens, but they all have a common thread, in that the focus is not simply on the food, but also on the fun and companionship to be found in sharing.

Even if you were not fortunate enough to have experienced the joy of learning to cook with a beloved family member or friend, there's no time like the present to change that! Create your own kitchen warmth, whip up something sweetly delicious and share it with the world, one person at a time. That way we can all have a store cupboard of luscious tastes and memories.

Terry's Chocolate-Orange Cake

The combination of chocolate and orange is, for me, one of the most delicious tastes around; when I was little and allowed to choose a bag of pick-and-mix sweets, I always tried to take as many orange creams as I could! Terry, who was a part of my life for several years, also loved this taste treat, so I devised this cake and topping for both of us. Although we have gone in different directions, he remains very special to me, and I will always treasure the time we had together. (And he was always so appreciative of everything I baked – even some of the more spectacular flops!)

375 ml (210 g) cake flour
5 ml baking powder
3 ml salt
90 g dark chocolate, chopped
60 ml hot and strong black coffee
125 g butter
375 ml (315 g) castor sugar
3 eggs, beaten
5 ml vanilla extract
125 ml sour cream
30 ml brandy
zest of 1 orange, finely grated

ORANGE BUTTERCREAM
60 g butter, softened
500 ml (260 g) icing sugar
1 egg yolk
60 ml fresh orange juice

Preheat the oven to 160 °C. Grease a medium loaf pan very well.

Sift together the flour, baking powder and salt, and set aside. Place the chocolate in a glass bowl over a pan of simmering water, and pour over the hot coffee. Stir until the mixture is smooth, and the chocolate has completely melted. Remove from the stove top and leave to cool.

Cream together the butter and castor sugar, then add the eggs and vanilla, and beat well to create a creamy and smooth batter. Stir in the cooled chocolate mixture. Add the flour mixture gradually to the batter, alternating with the sour cream. Lastly, stir in the brandy and about half of the orange zest. Spoon the batter into the prepared loaf pan and bake for 60–75 minutes until the cake has risen and a tester comes out clean. Leave to cool in the pan for 20 minutes, before turning out onto a wire rack to cool completely.

For the orange buttercream, combine the softened butter, half of the icing sugar, egg yolk and orange juice, to make a smooth mixture. Gradually add the remaining sugar and beat until fluffy. (You may need more icing sugar, if the mixture is too thin.) Spread the orange buttercream thickly over the top of the cooled cake, and sprinkle with the remaining orange zest. Store in an airtight container.

Serves 8–10

I have learnt not to worry about love, but to honour its coming with all my heart

ALICE WALKER

Aunt Eileen's Chocolate Cake

As a young girl, one of my favourite outings was a Sunday afternoon visit to Aunt Eileen and Uncle Bill at their wonderful Victorian home in Parkview. We always had to admire Uncle Bill's garden, his pride and joy – especially the hydrangeas that had a lush beauty and range of colour I have never seen since! Then we would take tea around the old dining room table, out of blue-and-white china cups. This cake was usually on the menu. Although the recipe is probably over 70 years old, I still make it often, and never without remembering Aunt Eileen herself, a woman of great charm, creativity and courage.

Life itself is the proper binge!

JULIA CHILD

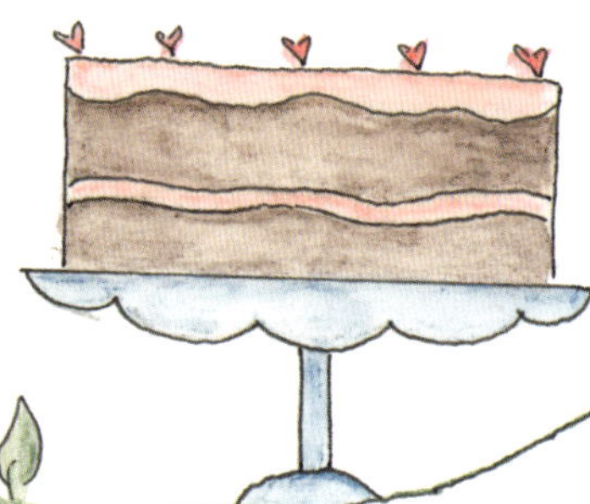

3 eggs, separated
200 ml (170 g) castor sugar
125 ml cold water
125 ml sunflower oil
5 ml vanilla extract
250 ml (140 g) cake flour, sifted
15 ml baking powder
60 ml cocoa
a pinch of salt

Preheat the oven to 180 °C. Grease 2 x 23-cm cake pans very well.

Beat the egg yolks and castor sugar together, until thick and pale. Combine the water, oil and vanilla, then slowly add to the egg mixture and beat for 7 minutes. Sift together the remaining dry ingredients and stir into the egg mixture until well combined. Beat the egg whites in a large bowl until they form stiff peaks then fold carefully into the cake mixture, until no white streaks remain.

Divide the batter between the cake pans. Bake for approximately 25 minutes, or until the cakes are well risen and a tester comes out clean. Leave to cool briefly then turn out onto a wire rack. When quite cold, fill and ice the top of the cake with Chocolate icing (see page 54).

Serves 8-10

Sticky Syrup and Ginger Cake

Ginger is, I think, one of those tastes usually acquired as an adult. When I was a child I absolutely hated it, even my mom's delicious homemade ginger beer. My father, on the other hand, would eat crystallised ginger with absolute delight! Now I like the taste a little more, especially when it comes in such a tasty package as this cake, which is soft and sticky, and really rather more like a pudding than a cake.

500 ml (280 g) cake flour
10 ml baking powder
3 ml salt
15 ml ground ginger
2 eggs
125 ml (100 g) light brown sugar
125 ml golden syrup, warmed
170 g butter, melted
125 ml sour cream
15 ml fresh ginger (optional)
additional syrup (optional)
icing sugar to sprinkle

You live and learn. At any rate, you live.

DOUGLAS ADAMS

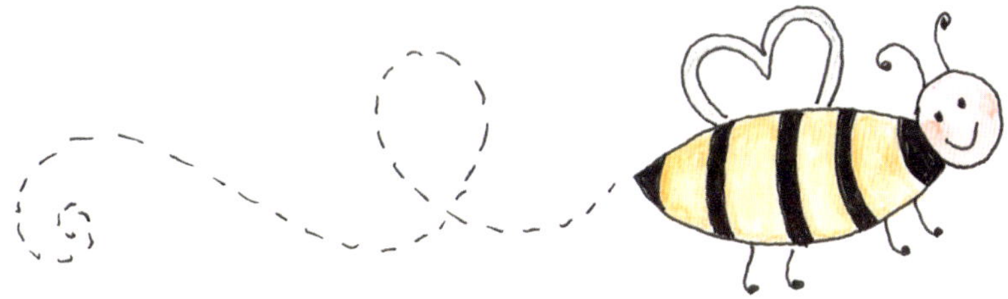

Preheat the oven to 180 °C. Grease a deep 25-cm round cake pan very well.

Sift together the flour, baking powder, salt and ground ginger, then set aside. In another bowl, beat together the eggs, light brown sugar, 125 ml syrup, melted butter and sour cream, until they are well combined. Mix the flour mixture with this batter, stirring well. Add the fresh ginger, if you are using it. Spread the batter in the prepared pan, then bake for 35–40 minutes, or until the cake is risen and firm, and a tester comes out clean.

Leave to cool briefly in the pan, then carefully turn the cake out onto a wire rack. Before serving you can brush a little extra warmed syrup over the top of the cake, or sprinkle it with icing sugar. Serve slices with whipped cream, and a little chopped crystallised ginger for real ginger lovers!

Serves 8–10

Devonshire Cream Cake

This is just such a classic taste to me – the sort of cake that we always had for special teas and occasions. These days you can buy it at many supermarkets and bakeries, but it just doesn't taste the same. The recipe is another old, traditional one that my mother often made when I was young; a classic sponge cake from England.

4 eggs, separated
45 ml water
250 ml (210 g) castor sugar
5 ml vanilla extract
250 ml (140 g) cake flour
23 ml cornflour
8 ml baking powder
3 ml salt

FILLING
250 ml cream
5 ml vanilla extract

GLAZE
45 ml cocoa powder
60 g butter
125 ml (65 g) icing sugar
30 ml milk

I'm making space for the unknown future to come and fill up my life with yet-to-come surprises.

ELIZABETH GILBERT

Preheat the oven to 180 °C. Grease 2 x 23-cm layer cake pans very well.

Using an electric mixer if possible, beat the egg yolks and water together in a large mixing bowl until they are thick and pale. Gradually beat in the castor sugar and vanilla. Sift the flour, cornflour, baking powder and salt together, then add to the egg yolk mixture, beating well. Whip the egg whites until stiff peaks form, then gently fold into the mixture, using a large metal spoon. Divide the batter between the cake pans. Bake for 10–15 minutes until risen and golden-brown, and a tester comes out clean. Leave to cool briefly before turning out onto a wire rack.

The cake must be completely cold before being filled and glazed, which should be done no more than 1 hour before you plan on serving the cake.

Whip the cream to soft peaks, and gently stir in the vanilla. Set aside while you make the glaze. Combine the cocoa, butter, icing sugar and milk in a small, heavy-bottomed saucepan, and stir until the butter has melted and the mixture is smooth. Remove from the heat, and leave to cool briefly. Spread the whipped cream between the cake layers, then drizzle the cooled glaze over the top of the cake, spreading it evenly. (It's fine if some drips down the sides!) Once filled and glazed, the cake is best eaten within a day or two.

Serves 6–8

Famous Lemon Drizzle Cake

When I lived in London, we were just around the corner from Tea Time – a very well-known tea shop close to Clapham Common. Many happy a day was spent there, enjoying tea and some of their wonderful cakes. I particularly enjoyed the lemon cake, because it always reminded me of a similar cake we used to have at home when I was young – soft, buttery sponge with the added tang of lemon glaze. No icing or other additions are needed – it's just perfect in its simplicity. Sometimes these are the best kind of things to bake – and eat!

2 juicy lemons
125 g butter, softened
200 ml (170 g) castor sugar
2 eggs
5 ml vanilla extract
375 ml (210 g) cake flour
10 ml baking powder
3 ml salt
125 ml milk
60 ml (50 g) castor sugar

A Proper Tea is much nicer than a Very Nearly Tea, which is one you forget about afterwards.

AA MILNE

Preheat the oven to 180 °C. Grease a medium loaf pan well.

First grate the zest of one of the lemons very finely, then juice both the lemons into a small bowl, and set aside.

Cream the butter and 200 ml sugar together well, then beat in the eggs and vanilla. Sift together the flour, baking powder and salt, then add to the butter mixture, alternately with the milk. Beat very well, to make a smooth and creamy batter. Stir in the lemon zest.

Pour into the prepared loaf pan and bake for approximately 45 minutes, until well risen and golden, and a tester comes out clean. While this is baking, mix the juice of the lemons with the 60 ml sugar. Remove the cake from the oven, and immediately prick the top all over with a fork. Pour the lemon juice mixture over the cake, so that the entire top is covered. Leave in the pan until quite cold – otherwise it might break – then turn out and serve.

This cake can be wrapped or kept in an airtight container in the fridge for a few days.

Makes 1 medium loaf

Devil's Food Cake with White Mountain Icing

The quintessential chocolate cake – make it for anyone, and they will love you forever! It just looks so gorgeous, dark and rich, and the fluffy, meringue-like icing (even though it is a bit of a pain to make) acts as the perfect counterpoint. This is one of those traditional recipes that never loses its charm.

125 g butter, softened
375 ml (315 g) castor sugar
2 eggs
5 ml bicarbonate of soda
125 ml (50 g) cocoa powder
a pinch of salt
375 ml (210 g) cake flour
5 ml baking powder
5 ml vanilla extract
200 ml water

ICING
3 egg whites
200 ml (170 g) castor sugar
3 ml salt
45 ml golden syrup
5 ml vanilla extract
fine desiccated coconut to sprinkle (optional)

I never worry about diets. The only carrots that interest me are the number you get in a diamond.

MAE WEST

Preheat the oven to 180 °C. Grease 2 x 23-cm round cake pans very well.

Cream the butter and 375 ml sugar together until light and fluffy, then add the eggs and beat well. Sift together the bicarbonate of soda, cocoa powder, salt, flour and baking powder, then add to the creamed mixture. Lastly, stir in the vanilla and water, and beat well for 2 minutes. Divide the batter between the prepared cake pans, and bake for 30–35 minutes, until well-risen and a tester comes out clean. Turn out onto a wire rack and leave to cool.

For the icing, combine the egg whites, 200 ml sugar, salt and syrup in a large glass bowl set over a pan of gently simmering water. Using an electric beater, whisk the mixture until the egg whites are stiff and glossy – this takes around 5–7 minutes. Remove from the heat, stir in the vanilla, then ice the cake immediately, between the layers and on top. Sprinkle with coconut, if you like. Once the cake has been iced, serve within a few hours.

Serves 8–10

Sunday Night Cake with Butterscotch Sauce

This is a simple butter cake, but the flavour is divine, and topped with butterscotch sauce it becomes a cake to be reckoned with! An ideal 'pudding' cake after a light supper – although it can be served for tea, too. The original recipe, which I have changed somewhat, comes from a wonderful American cook called Edna Lewis, who wrote beautifully about the foods of her childhood, growing up in an extended family in the American South. Just reading about her fried chicken or peach ice cream is enough to make the mouth water. (Please note that you do need a fairly large and deep cake pan for this, otherwise the batter tends to overflow!)

450 ml (250 g) cake flour
10 ml baking powder
5 ml salt
3 ml ground cinnamon
165 g butter, softened
200 ml (170 g) castor sugar
125 ml (100 g) light brown sugar
3 eggs
5 ml vanilla extract
250 ml buttermilk

BUTTERSCOTCH SAUCE
250 ml (200 g) light brown sugar
80 ml cream
75 g butter
5 ml vanilla extract

Preheat the oven to 180 °C. Grease a round or square 25-cm cake pan very well.

Sift together the flour, baking powder, salt and cinnamon in a large bowl. In another bowl, cream together the softened butter and both sugars until light and fluffy. Stir in the eggs, one at a time, and lastly add the vanilla. Add the dry ingredients gradually to the butter mixture, alternating with the buttermilk, and beat until smooth and thick. Pour the batter into the prepared pan, spreading evenly.

Bake for 30–35 minutes, or until the cake has risen and a tester comes out clean. Leave to cool in the pan, then carefully turn out onto a wire rack until cold.

To make the sauce, combine all the ingredients in a heavy-bottomed saucepan over a low heat, and stir until the sugar has dissolved and the butter melted. Bring to a gentle boil, stirring all the time, boil for 3 minutes then remove from the heat and leave to cool a bit. Serve warm over squares or wedges of the cake.

Serves 12–16

Knowledge is limited. Imagination encircles the world.

ALBERT EINSTEIN

The Taste of Memory

One of my most treasured cookbooks is a handmade one, in a blue ringbinder file, that my mother gave me when I was in my early twenties. Handwritten with little illustrations and quotes, it contains all the favourite recipes she made when I was growing up – the same recipes with which I started my own cooking journey – and is the inspiration behind many of the goodies in this book!

My mom was given a similar recipe scrapbook before her marriage, by her mother (my grandmother), although hers was slightly different in that it contained recipes collected from family and friends; each recipe presented in its own way, some typed, others handwritten, yet others clipped from newspapers or magazines. It was a wonderful way to remember special people and good times shared, although, sadly, it went missing some years ago after a house move.

My maternal granny died much too young, when I was barely two years' old, so any memories I have of her come only from my mom and the stories she has told me. She said that my grandmother was a good and competent cook, but it was not one of her passions; she had too many interests, such as science, art and writing poetry. As for my great-grandmother, I wish I had a handwritten cookbook from her, as I think it would make for both fascinating and delicious reading!

Minnie Dale Ritchie, born Thwaite, originally from England, met my great-grandfather, who was a Canadian military doctor, on a ship bound for the Cape from India. After they married they settled in Queenstown, in the Eastern Cape. My granny, Mary Frances Isabella, was their seventh child, born in 1903. My great aunt

Emily was their first child, and in between they had five strapping sons. I imagine Minnie must have been rather busy in the kitchen, providing meals for that lot. (My mother does have one cookbook that was apparently passed down from her, an edition of *Mrs Beeton's Book of Household Management* that predates the First World War.)

I'm sure their food must have been simple, hearty and good. My grandmother used to go out with her father in his horse-drawn trap when he visited patients, and often he would be paid in kind, rather than cash, with fresh meat, eggs, vegetables and the like. How I would love to have been a guest at that dinner table, in a simpler, more gentle age.

I often think about the women who have lived their lives before me, whose lifelines and blood I share – we may be separated by years and an ever-changing world, but the basic, true and good things don't change, such as cooking and sharing with our loved ones. When we are in our kitchens, preparing meals, whatever our heritage may be – Portuguese, Afrikaans, Xhosa, Scottish, Greek – we are part of a unique legacy of taste, which is something to treasure and celebrate every day.

OPPOSITE: My mom, the little dancer

LEFT: Grandma, great-aunt and great-grandma, Queenstown, 1932

Rosie's Best Scones

Scones are endlessly versatile, yet simple and quick to make. I love them – both making and eating – piled high with thick farm cream and strawberry preserves, or buttered, with lots of grated cheese or honey. This recipe, which has also been handed down through the family, is for a traditional scone, flaky and soft. You can leave out the sugar if you are planning to serve the scones with savoury toppings. The same applies to the raisins, or you can substitute them with currants or sultanas.

500 ml (280 g) cake flour, sifted
15 ml baking powder
3 ml salt
30 ml castor sugar
125 g butter, cubed
125 ml (75 g) raisins
1 egg
125 ml milk

Preheat the oven to 200 °C. Grease a baking sheet very well.

Sift the dry ingredients together in a large bowl. Rub in the butter until the mixture resembles fine breadcrumbs. Stir in the raisins. Beat the egg and milk together, then mix into the flour mixture to form a soft, but not sticky, dough. Turn out onto a floured board, and press the dough out until it is about 2.5 cm thick. (Don't handle the dough too much, or the scones will be heavy.)

Cut out rounds with a cutter or glass, then place on the prepared baking sheet. Bake for about 12 minutes until well-risen and golden-brown. Best served fresh.

Makes 10–15

How many cares one loses when one decides not to be something, but to be someone.

GABRIELLE (COCO) CHANEL

Chelsea Garden Scones

When I lived in London there was a small bakery near our flat in Clapham; rather unprepossessing in appearance, a small sliver of a shop with a handful of tables, but they turned out an endless stream of delicious baked goods. There was nothing better than looking out on a grey London winter day while munching on one of their Sticky Chelsea Buns – hot, flaky and bursting with cinnamon and raisins. This is a simpler version I developed – no yeast, but just as tasty for tea – or lovely for breakfast or brunch.

500 ml (280 g) cake flour, sifted
20 ml baking powder
3 ml salt
60 g butter, softened
1 egg
250 ml buttermilk

FILLING
30 g butter
125 ml (100 g) brown sugar
5 ml ground cinnamon
125 ml (75 g) raisins

VANILLA GLAZE
125 ml (65 g) icing sugar
3 ml vanilla extract
a little milk

Preheat the oven to 220 °C. Line a large baking sheet with baking paper and grease lightly.

Combine the flour, baking powder and salt in a large bowl. Rub in the softened butter lightly with your fingertips.

Beat the egg and buttermilk together, then mix into the flour mixture to form a soft, but not sticky dough. On a floured board, pat the dough out to form a rectangle approximately 20 x 25 x 1 cm-thick.

To make the filling beat the butter, brown sugar and cinnamon together and spread over the dough. Sprinkle with the raisins. Starting at the long side, roll up like a Swiss roll, then cut into 10–12 slices. Place the slices on the prepared baking sheet and bake for 15 minutes until risen and golden. Leave to cool briefly on a wire rack.

For the vanilla glaze, combine the icing sugar and vanilla with sufficient milk to create a fairly runny consistency. Drizzle the glaze over the scone slices once they have cooled. Best served fresh!

Makes 10–12

Life itself is full, not only of charm and warmth and comfort but of sorrow and tears. But whether we are happy or sad, we must be fed.

LAURIE COLWIN

Buttermilk Custard Pie

When I was in my early teens we had an Afrikaans and Home Economics teacher called Miss Joubert – of course she seemed incredibly ancient to us, but she was probably only in her fifties. She was one of those teachers who was not only filled with enthusiasm for her subject, but also possessed of a great deal of empathy and understanding for her students. Because I already loved cooking – although my sewing skills were less well developed – I found her lessons enormous fun. She had grown up on a dairy farm in the Cape, and this buttermilk pie was her recipe; apparently there was always plenty of buttermilk around on a dairy farm! She said it was nicer than milk tart – and in some ways I think I agree with her. I still use some of the recipes written out in my exercise book from those carefree days: it's comforting to continue something through the years. You will need a 23-cm baked pie crust for this recipe; use your own favourite, or a store-bought shortcrust pastry. Another note about the buttermilk – it needs to be fairly thin and smooth, not the thick, lumpy kind. Woolworths makes a good one.

The good teachers fill you up with hope and shower you with a thousand reasons to embrace all aspects of life.

PAT CONROY

1 x 23-cm baked pie crust (fairly deep)
250 ml (210 g) castor sugar
60 g butter, softened
45 ml cake flour, sifted
3 ml salt
4 eggs, separated
500 ml buttermilk
5 ml vanilla extract
10 ml ground cinnamon

Preheat the oven to 200 °C. Place the pie crust on a baking sheet.

Cream the sugar and butter together in a large bowl, then blend in the flour and salt, followed by the egg yolks. Beat well until the mixture is smooth. Stir in the buttermilk and vanilla extract.

Beat the egg whites until they are stiff but not dry, then gently fold them into the buttermilk mixture. Pour the mixture into the pie crust, and sprinkle with the cinnamon. Bake for 10 minutes, then reduce the oven temperature to 190 °C and continue baking for another 25 minutes, or until the custard is set and golden-brown. (The top of the pie may crack a little, which is fine.)
Leave to cool completely before serving.

Serves 6–8

Chocolate Truffle Tart for Michelle

Michelle, a beloved friend lost too soon, admitted to being one of the world's worst cooks. (I think she survived on coffee and microwave-baked potatoes!) She adored chocolate and told me about a chocolate tart she often had as a child. When I made this one for her, she said it was like taking a bite of the past. It is quick and easy to make and always reminds me of her.

- 125 g butter, softened
- 200 ml (170 g) castor sugar
- 2 eggs, separated
- 90 g dark chocolate, chopped
- 125 ml (70 g) cake flour
- 5 ml vanilla extract
- a pinch of salt
- fresh raspberries or strawberries, to garnish (optional)

Preheat the oven to 160 °C. Grease a fairly deep 20-cm pie dish or tart pan well.

Cream the butter and sugar together well, then beat in the egg yolks, one at a time. Melt the chocolate in a small bowl set over a pan of hot water. Once it has completely melted, leave to cool slightly before stirring it into the butter mixture. Beat the flour, vanilla and salt into the mixture until smooth.

In a separate bowl, beat the egg whites until stiff but not dry. Fold them gently and thoroughly into the chocolate mixture until no streaks of white remain. Spread the batter in the prepared pie or tart dish and bake for about 30 minutes – it will rise slightly. Leave to cool in the dish.

Serve chilled, preferably, with lots of whipped cream. A few fresh raspberries or strawberries also make a charming garnish.

Serves 6–8

A friend knows the song in my heart, and sings it to me when my memory fails.

DONNA ROBERTS

Mom's Best Shortbread Cookies

Simple and utterly delicious, this recipe from my mom has been around forever! We used to make endless batches of them as Christmas gifts, decorating them in all sorts of ways, with cherries, chocolate vermicelli, silver balls and hundreds-and-thousands, or cutting them into shapes and icing them to look like snowmen, bells and Christmas trees. It's another wonderful recipe to make with children – even if it's quite a task to stop them from eating half of the cookies before they have even cooled down! This, to me, is one of those 'forever' recipes that define simple home baking.

125 g butter, softened
125 ml (105 g) castor sugar
1 egg
5 ml vanilla extract
250 ml (140 g) cake flour, sifted
3 ml baking powder

Preheat the oven to 180 °C. Grease a large baking sheet well.

Cream the butter and sugar together well. Mix in the egg and vanilla. In another bowl, combine the flour and baking powder, then stir into the creamed mixture until it becomes a soft dough. Wrap the dough in greaseproof paper, then refrigerate for 30 minutes.

On a floured surface, roll the dough out until it is no more than 5 mm thick, then cut into the desired shapes. If you like, decorate with cherries, nuts, chocolate chips, etc. Place on the baking sheet and bake for 10-15 minutes, until the biscuits are golden. Leave to cool on a wire rack. If you are icing them, wait until they are completely cold.

Makes 20–25

I'm a rich man. To have everything you need is the definition of affluence.

LEE CHILD

Hungarian Apricot Tart with Vanilla Glaze

When I was growing up, the Hobergs were our next door neighbours – a German family with four impossibly blonde, tall and beautiful children. Their mother, Aunty Hoberg as I always called her, was a wonderful cook with a warm and welcoming kitchen that I can still see in my mind's eye. This apricot tart was originally her recipe, which she gave to my mom over 40 years ago. (The vanilla glaze is my addition, but you can leave it off if you prefer.) It's a deliciously simple tea time bake, although it also makes a good dessert, warmed and served with cream.

125 g butter, softened
60 ml (50 g) castor sugar
30 ml sunflower oil
5 ml vanilla extract
1 egg, beaten
500 ml (280 g) cake flour
3 ml salt
10 ml baking powder
250 ml (150 g) apricot preserve

VANILLA GLAZE
125 ml (65 g) icing sugar
3 ml vanilla extract
warm water

One's home is like a delicious piece of pie you order in a restaurant on a country road one cosy evening – the best piece of pie you have eaten in your life and can never really find again ...

LEMONY SNICKET

Preheat the oven to 150 °C. Grease a 23-cm square baking pan well.

Cream the butter and castor sugar together well, then add the oil and vanilla. Stir in the egg, followed by the flour, salt and baking powder, to form a soft dough. Divide the dough in half, then press one half evenly over the base of the prepared pan. Spread with the apricot preserve. Grate the rest of the dough over the top. Bake for around 40–45 minutes, until the topping is golden-brown.

To make the vanilla glaze, in a bowl mix together the icing sugar, vanilla and sufficient warm water to make a smooth, pourable mixture.

Leave the tart to cool in the pan, before drizzling over the vanilla glaze. Cut into squares, and store in an airtight container.

Makes 16 squares

Jungle Bungles

When I was little, my Mom used to bake a version of these in a tray and cut them into bars or squares. I actually prefer these cookies – although the recipe is basically the same – baked in a baking tray. It's just such a simple, homely recipe, guaranteed to please and bring a smile: sweet nostalgia at its best!

250 ml (140 g) cake flour
250 ml (80 g) desiccated coconut
160 ml (130 g) brown sugar
250 ml (80 g) rolled oats
125 g butter
60 ml golden syrup
5 ml vanilla extract
5 ml bicarbonate of soda dissolved in 30 ml boiling water

Preheat the oven to 160 °C. Line a large (20 x 30 cm) baking dish with baking paper. (If you don't have a large dish you will have to use 2 smaller dishes, or make 2 batches.)

Mix the flour, coconut, sugar and oats together in a large bowl. In a saucepan, melt the butter with the syrup and vanilla over a gentle heat. Stir in the bicarbonate of soda dissolved in boiling water. Pour the butter mixture over the dry ingredients, and mix quickly until well combined.

Place balls of the mixture on the prepared baking tray(s), leaving sufficient space for spreading. Flatten the balls slightly with a fork and bake for 15–20 minutes until golden-brown. Leave to cool on a wire rack, then store in an airtight container to prevent them from hardening.

Makes 20–25

If God had intended us to follow recipes, He wouldn't have given us grandmothers.

LINDA HENLEY

Morning Glory Muffins

Even the name makes you want to get out of bed for one of these moist muffins, packed with fruit flavour. (Although they probably sound healthier than they actually are!) A friend of mine ate these in a small cafe in New England, when she was on holiday there, and raved about them, so I searched for the recipe, but eventually created my own version, which she says is as good as the original!

450 ml (250 g) cake flour
5 ml baking powder
3 ml salt
5 ml ground cinnamon
125 ml (40 g) desiccated coconut
250 ml (210 g) castor sugar
2 eggs
125 ml sunflower oil
5 ml vanilla extract
250 ml apple, peeled and grated
125 ml carrot, peeled and grated
125 ml (75 g) raisins

Preheat the oven to 180 °C. Grease a regular sized, 12-cup muffin pan well, or use paper cases.

In a large bowl, mix together the flour, baking powder, salt, cinnamon and coconut. In another bowl, beat the sugar, eggs, oil and vanilla together until thick and creamy. Stir into the dry ingredients, then mix in the apple, carrot and raisins until blended, but do not overmix.

Fill the muffin cups three-quarters full with the mixture. Bake for 25–30 minutes, until risen and golden-brown. Leave to cool in the pan for 5 minutes before turning out onto a wire rack. The muffins can be stored in an airtight container for a couple of days.

Makes 12

It's better to be absolutely ridiculous than absolutely boring!

MARILYN MONROE

Being at home

I think someone once said that 'home', rather than 'love', was one of the most beautiful words in the English language. In many ways that is true, for the very word conjures up an image of warmth, security and peace. Some of us have been lucky enough to experience that in our homes of origin, while others have to wait a little longer to find their true home – and yet others are still searching.

For me, although it is a bit of a cliché, the kitchen really is the warm heart of a home. Food is a daily necessity, yes, but in a happy home it is far more than that – it is the sharing of the moments of our lives.

Perhaps that's why so many of us are returning to the traditions of baking and cooking, because they remind us of where we came from, and where we are going, and in that way we can nurture those who share this journey with us.

Home … wasn't a place, but a moment, and then another, building on each other like bricks to create a solid shelter that you took with you your entire life, wherever you might go.

SARAH DESSEN

Creamy Rice Pudding

Rice pudding has to be one of those universal tastes – worldwide comfort food. We often had it during the cold months when I was growing up, a fairly plain and unadorned version. Since then I have eaten it in other incarnations – a Middle Eastern version flavoured with rose water, which was surprisingly delicious, or a cold Greek rice pudding, tasting of almonds. In England it is often served with a hefty spoon of strawberry jam. This recipe is a hybrid of tastes – you can use any rice you prefer, but I usually choose either Basmati or Jasmine rice, as they cook up soft and white, with a very delicate fragrance.

- 4 eggs, separated
- 125 ml (105 g) castor sugar
- 5 ml vanilla extract
- 250 ml milk
- 250 ml whipping cream
- 125 ml (70 g) cake flour
- 5 ml baking powder
- 3 ml salt
- 500 ml cooked rice, cooled
- 30 g butter, melted
- ground cinnamon to sprinkle
- apricot or strawberry preserve (optional)

Preheat the oven to 180 °C. Grease a medium oval or rectangular baking dish well.

Beat the egg yolks, sugar and vanilla together well. Stir in the milk and cream. Sift together the flour, baking powder and salt and add it to the egg yolk mixture, mixing until smooth. Add the cold cooked rice and melted butter. Lastly, beat the egg whites until stiff, but not dry, and gently fold into the mixture. Pour into the prepared baking dish, and sprinkle with cinnamon.

Bake for 40–50 minutes, or until the pudding is set and golden-brown. This pudding is nicest served hot, with a hefty dollop of fruit preserve (if you like) or just with cream or custard, but it also tastes good cold.

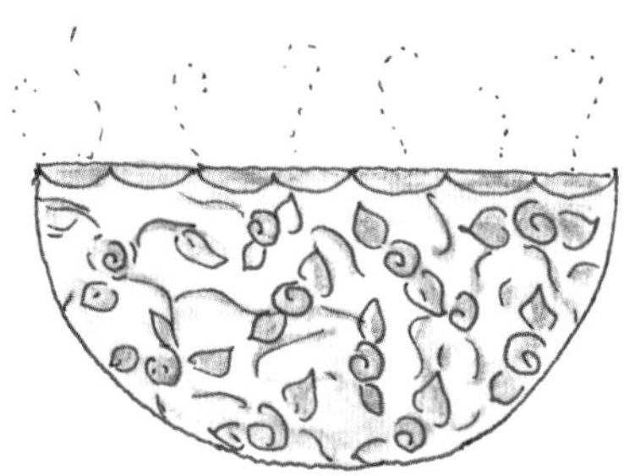

Serves 6

Great Grandma's Queen of Puddings

This recipe is allegedly one used by my great-grandmother over 100 years ago – although it is so widely popular that she certainly would not have laid claim to it. Still, I like to think of her serving this up to her hungry brood of seven children on a cold winter's night in the Eastern Cape. It was one of my favourite puddings when I was a child, and I loved the blue speckled earthenware dish my mom used to bake it in. Comfort food at its best! It must be served with a jug of cream or thick vanilla custard. You may use any jam you like – apricot is good – or even marmalade.

375 ml milk
2 eggs, separated
60 ml (50 g) castor sugar
330 ml (80 g) fresh breadcrumbs
5 ml vanilla extract
strawberry or raspberry jam, for spreading

Preheat the oven to 180 °C. Grease an oval or rectangular baking dish well.

Heat the milk. In a bowl, beat the egg yolks well with 30 ml of the sugar. Add the milk to the yolks and stir well. Place the breadcrumbs in another bowl, then pour the egg yolk mixture over the breadcrumbs and stir in the vanilla. Pour into the prepared dish and bake for 30–35 minutes.

Remove from the oven, and reduce the heat to 160 °C. Spread a thin layer of jam over the pudding. Whisk the egg whites until stiff but not grainy, then fold in the remaining sugar. Pile decoratively on top of the pudding, and bake again for about 15 minutes, until the meringue topping is set and golden.

Serves 4

Contentment is a constant feast.

SCOTTISH PROVERB

Chocolate Fudge Pudding

This is the perfect antidote to a miserable winter evening, when some chocolate therapy is needed. My mother has been making this for years; when she worked as a cook at a retreat centre in England it was vastly popular and became known, accurately if inelegantly, as 'squashy bottom pudding'!

125 g butter, softened
125 ml (105 g) castor sugar
2 eggs
310 ml (175 g) self-raising flour, sifted
45 ml cocoa powder
a pinch of salt
15–30 ml milk
5 ml vanilla extract

SAUCE
30 ml cocoa powder
60 ml (50 g) brown sugar
375 ml boiling water

Preheat the oven to 180 °C. Grease a fairly large oval or rectangular baking dish.

Cream the butter and castor sugar together well. Add the eggs and beat again. In another bowl, sift together the flour, cocoa powder and salt. Mix the butter mixture with the flour mixture, then stir in the milk and vanilla. Spread the batter in the prepared baking dish.

To make the sauce, place the cocoa powder and brown sugar in a bowl, pour over the boiling water and stir until the mixture has dissolved. Carefully pour this mixture over the unbaked pudding in the dish.

Bake for around 40 minutes, until the pudding is well risen. (A layer of fudge sauce will have formed under the batter.) This dessert must be served piping hot, with lots of thick cream or custard. (I sometimes add 30 ml brandy or coffee liqueur to the sauce mixture, for a little extra oomph!)

Serves 4–6 (or 2 greedy people!)

Date and Nut Pudding with Whisky Sauce

Here is another 'winter' recipe, which makes the cold almost worthwhile. This is often also called tipsy tart, and there are a number of different recipes out there, but this version is a classic, as made by my family for years. The whisky sauce is my addition; you should really try it, even if you think you don't like whisky. A friend of mine always makes hers with Southern Comfort, which is yet another good idea! As an alternative to a single large pudding, divide the batter among six jumbo muffin cups, and bake individual puddings. (You can omit the water bath in this instance.) Serve each individual pudding with a generous quantity of the sauce spooned over the top.

250 g pitted dates, chopped finely
125 g butter
5 ml bicarbonate of soda
250 ml boiling water
375 ml (210 g) cake flour
5 ml baking powder
2 eggs
5 ml vanilla extract
125 ml (100 g) light brown sugar
125 ml (75 g) chopped pecan nuts

WHISKY SAUCE
80 ml (70 g) castor sugar
60 g butter
125 ml cream
45 ml whisky (or alcohol of your choice)

Preheat the oven to 180 °C. Grease a medium oval or rectangular baking dish very well.

Place the dates, 125 g butter and bicarbonate of soda in a large bowl, then pour over the boiling water. Leave to stand until the butter has melted and the mixture has cooled.

Sift together the flour and baking powder, and set aside. In another bowl, beat the eggs, vanilla and light brown sugar together until smooth. Stir in the cooled date mixture, followed by the flour and beat well. Finally, mix in the nuts. Pour the batter into the prepared baking dish, then stand the dish in a roasting pan half-filled with water. Bake for 35–40 minutes, or until the pudding has risen and you've tested for 'done-ness'.

To make the whisky sauce, combine the castor sugar, 60 g butter and cream in a small saucepan. Heat gently, stirring, until the butter has melted and the sauce is smooth. Stir in the whisky. Spoon over the date pudding.

Serve as soon as possible, with a little cream on the side!

Serves 6

The past is a ghost, the future is a dream,
and all we ever have is now.

BILL COSBY

Lemon Delicious Pudding

Comfort food again, in the guise of a pudding that magically separates into two layers, the top light and cakelike, the bottom a creamy lemon custard. I can honestly say I have never met anyone who doesn't like this, even those who claim not to care much for lemons. Another perfect winter pudding, which simply must be served with a jug of thick cream.

1 large lemon
125 g butter, softened
250 ml (210 g) castor sugar
15 ml boiling water
4 eggs, separated
250 ml (140 g) cake flour
500 ml milk

Preheat the oven to 180 °C. Grease a large baking dish well.

Grate the lemon rind very finely and squeeze the juice into a cup. In a bowl, cream the butter, sugar and boiling water together. Add the egg yolks and grated lemon rind; then slowly stir in the flour, and beat well. Mix in the milk followed by the lemon juice, to make a smooth batter.

Whip the egg whites until stiff but not dry, then fold into the batter gently until they are thoroughly incorporated. Pour the mixture into the prepared dish.

Stand the dish in a large roasting pan half-filled with warm water, and bake for approximately 45 minutes, until risen and golden. Serve warm.

Serves 6

Be who you are and say what you feel, because those who mind don't matter, and those who matter don't mind.

DR SEUSS

Earth Angels

I have always believed in angels, and feel sure that we are surrounded by unseen forces for good, protecting and guiding us. Equally as powerful are the earth angels – those who make a difference in our lives, often simply by being there. They can be family, friends, co-workers, someone on the bus; there is something about them that just inspires and empowers us.

One of my earth angels was my uncle Frank, my mom's older brother. He was just there, throughout my childhood, warm, friendly, a comforting and loving presence to everyone who came in contact with him. He also noticed things that others overlooked. For example, when our families went out to dinner, he knew that my favourite dessert was crêpes suzette, but it was always only prepared for two, because it was quite a production to make. No-one else in the family liked it, so I could not order it until one New Year's Eve dinner when he announced, 'Gail and I are going to have our crêpes suzette.' To this day I don't know if he even liked them, but he wanted to make me happy. And he ordered them at every special dinner after that.

It's not a big thing, I know, but it resonates with me to this day. My only regret is that I never had the opportunity to thank him for the presence he was in my life. He died too young, before his fiftieth birthday, but even when he was very ill, and we visited him in hospital, there was no self-pity or sadness. He was always more concerned about us, or telling silly jokes.

At his funeral, a colleague said: 'Frank's heart was like a Putco bus – always room for just one more.' What a lovely epitaph. I hope one day I get to make some crêpes suzette for him again.

LEFT: Uncle Frank, one of the good guys

Uncle Frank's Crêpes Suzette

Here is my simpler interpretation of the classic French dessert, made with love and memory. If you like, you can still flame the dish with a little brandy just as you are serving it, although I think it's gilding the lily. And yes, I know the crêpes have a lot of eggs in them, but that is what makes them soft, golden and delicious!

CRÊPES	SAUCE
210 ml (175 g) cake flour	60 g butter
3 ml salt	60 ml (50 g) castor sugar
3 eggs	250 ml fresh orange juice
250 ml milk	juice of 1 small lemon
125 ml water	60 ml brandy
15 ml melted butter	zest of 1 orange (optional)

To make the crêpes, sift the flour and salt into a large bowl. In another bowl, beat the eggs well then gradually add both the milk and water. Pour the egg mixture into the dry ingredients and beat very well, until the mixture is smooth, like pouring cream. Stir in the melted butter. Leave the batter to stand for at least 1 hour before making the crêpes.

Using paper towel with a little cooking oil on it, wipe out a small, heavy-bottomed frying pan, approximately 15 cm in diameter. Heat until a drop of water sizzles in the pan, then pour just enough batter into the pan to thinly coat the base and cook until pale golden-brown on one side. Flip and cook the other side. Remove the crêpe from the pan, fold into quarters and place on a covered plate. Repeat until all the batter is used up.
(This should be sufficient for 12–16 crêpes.)

About 30 minutes before serving, preheat the oven to 180 °C. Arrange the crêpes in a shallow, rectangular baking dish. For the sauce, melt the butter and sugar together in a saucepan over low heat until the sugar has completely dissolved. Stir in the orange and lemon juice, followed by the brandy. Simmer for at least 5 minutes. Remove from the heat and pour over the crêpes. Bake for approximately 15 minutes, or until the crêpes are heated through, and the sauce is bubbly. Sprinkle with the orange zest, if using, and serve piping hot.

Serves 6–8

When I walk, I walk with you.
Where I go, you're with me always.

ALICE HOFFMAN

Super Quick Herb, Cheese and Wine Bread

I've always loved making quick breads. As a rule, they offer almost instant gratification with very little effort, and they usually taste good to boot. This bread has undergone a number of changes since I first started making it some years ago – and now I think it's really delicious, served in a number of different ways. With a chunky soup and salad it makes a wonderful light meal, or you can serve it on the side at a braai, or as an accompaniment to a hearty stew. As with most quick breads, this really should be eaten on the day it is made.

Always try to keep a patch of sky above your life.

MARCEL PROUST

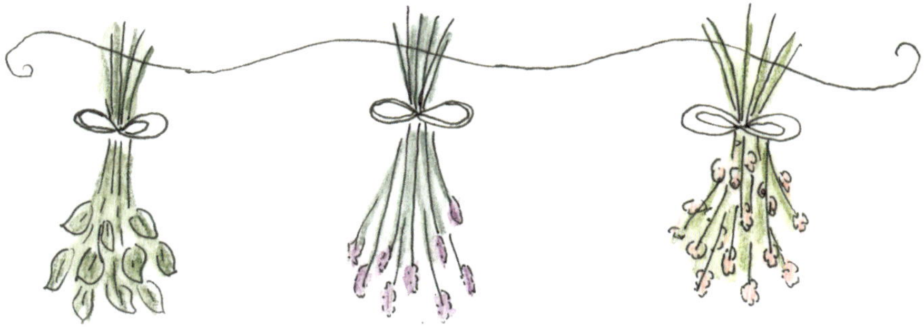

500 ml (280 g) cake flour
15 ml baking powder
5 ml salt
125 ml (50 g) grated Cheddar cheese
30 ml finely grated onion
90 g butter, cubed
1 egg
125 ml milk
125 ml dry white wine
30 ml finely chopped fresh parsley

Preheat the oven to 190 °C. Grease a square 23-cm baking pan well.

Sift together the flour, baking powder and salt in a large bowl. Stir in half the grated cheese, and the grated onion. Rub in the butter with your fingertips, until the mixture resembles fine breadcrumbs.

In a separate bowl, combine the egg, milk and wine and beat briefly. Make a well in the centre of the flour mixture, and pour the egg mixture into it. Mix briefly but thoroughly, taking care not to overbeat. Stir in the parsley. Spread the batter in the prepared pan, then sprinkle with the remaining cheese.

Bake for 25–30 minutes, or until the top is golden-brown and a tester comes out clean. Leave to cool briefly in the pan, then cut into squares and serve warm.

Makes 9 large squares

Julia's Feta Fritters

Julia came to work for us when I was about 19, and she remained a key figure in my life until she passed away, just a few years ago. She and my mother were very similar in many ways – small, determined women who confronted sometimes difficult challenges with grace and courage. The African saying 'you strike a woman, you strike a rock' definitely applied. 'Jools', as I always called her, had previously worked for a Greek family, and she made the most wonderful food, including the best Greek salad I have ever tasted. These little feta fritters were another of her favourites – lovely as a snack, or as a side dish with a Greek meal (or any meal, for that matter). She always used mint, because she loved it, but I sometimes use oregano instead.

Julia, a dear friend, probably still cooking and knitting up a storm in heaven!

Time doesn't take away from friendship.
Nor does separation.

TENNESSEE WILLIAMS

125 g feta cheese, finely crumbled
half a small onion, finely chopped
5 ml minced garlic
30 ml chopped fresh mint
160 ml (90 g) cake flour
5 ml salt
cold water
1 egg white
olive oil for frying

Combine the feta, onion, garlic and mint in a bowl. Sprinkle over 30 ml of the flour. In another bowl, mix together the remaining flour and salt, with sufficient cold water to make a fairly thick paste. Beat the egg white until stiff, then fold it into the flour paste. Stir this into the feta mixture.

Heat a shallow layer of olive oil in a heavy-bottomed frying pan. Drop generous tablespoonfuls of the mixture in the pan and fry until golden-brown on both sides. Drain well on paper towel, and serve warm, if possible.

Makes 12–15

Little Sausage, Apple and Sage Rolls

A woman I know makes sausage rolls – and that is all she makes. She's become pretty famous for them, and is kept very busy rolling out a continual stream of orders. Quite justifiably so, for they are the most delicious sausage rolls I have ever eaten. Naturally, she will not part with her recipe, but I like to think that this one is also pretty good. Normally I am not a big fan of making pastry, but this recipe is a really quick and easy one.

FILLING

400 g beef sausages (or a mixture of pork and beef)
10 ml dried sage
5 ml minced garlic
1 small apple, peeled and grated
30 ml minced onion
10 ml prepared Dijon mustard
1 egg
salt and pepper to taste

PASTRY

500 ml (280 g) cake flour
3 ml salt
250 g cold butter
250 g tub cream cheese
a little egg yolk or milk

I am not a glutton. I am an explorer of food.

IRMA BOMBECK

Make the filling first. Squeeze the sausages out of their skins into a large bowl. Then add all the remaining ingredients, and mix very well; this is a messy business and I find it best to use my hands! Leave the filling in the fridge to firm up while you prepare the pastry.

Preheat the oven to 200 °C. Line a large baking sheet with baking paper.

In a large bowl, combine the flour and salt. Grate the cold butter into the flour mixture, then using your fingertips, rub it in until the mixture resembles breadcrumbs. Add the cream cheese, then mix to a soft, but manageable, dough. (If the dough is too soft, add a little more flour.) Leave to chill in the fridge for 30 minutes.

Divide the dough in half. Turn each half out onto a floured surface, and roll out to make a rectangle of around 28 x 14 cm each. Trim the edges. Divide the sausage filling into two, and form each into a long, thin roll, just a little shorter than the long edge of the pastry. Place the filling onto one side of the pastry rectangle, and fold the other side over, pressing down with a fork to seal. (The filling must be totally enclosed.) Do the same with the second batch of pastry and filling.

Arrange the two sausage rolls on the prepared baking sheet. Brush with a little egg yolk or milk, and cut several shallow slits into the top of the rolls. Bake for 30–40 minutes, until the pastry is golden-brown. Leave to cool on the sheet, then cut into 6 smaller rolls each and either serve hot, or cool completely to serve later.

Makes 12 medium sausage rolls

Emily's Cheese Straws

My great-aunt Emily, my granny's sister, was a brilliant, artistic woman who lived a long and creative life in her wonderful Victorian house in Queenstown. I remember visiting that house as a young girl and, most especially, I remember her African Grey parrot, a lovely and chatty bird, who was known to warble 'Coming through the Rye' on occasion. Aunt Emily apparently always kept a stash of crisp and delicious cheese straws in a tin; I am not sure if this recipe, which my mother taught me when I was really young, was hers, but in my mind they have always been Aunt Emily's Cheese Straws.

200 ml (110 g) cake flour
5 ml salt
5 ml paprika
200 ml (75 g) grated Cheddar cheese
60 g cold butter
1 egg yolk

Preheat the oven to 220 °C. Grease a large baking sheet well.

In a medium bowl, mix together the flour, salt, paprika and cheese. Grate the cold butter into the flour mixture, then rub in well with your fingertips. Stir in the egg yolk to form a stiff dough (you will probably need to add a few teaspoons of cold water). Roll the dough out on a floured surface until around 4 mm thick, then cut into strips. (I find 1 x 8 cm works well.) Place the strips on the prepared baking sheet and bake for 10–15 minutes until lightly browned. Leave to cool on a wire rack and store in a tin.

Makes 25–30

The bond that links a true family is not one of blood, but of respect and joy in each other's life.

RICHARD BACH

Heavenly Bread Puffs

If angels ate anything as ordinary as bread, it would have to be these, as they are just so light and ethereal! My mother has been making them for as long as I can remember, and they were my first effort at bread-making, too. They are best served warm with butter or with cheese, filled with tuna or chicken salad, sliced and topped with cream cheese and slivers of smoked salmon … you get the idea! They taste wonderful with soup. Alternatively, make them in those mini muffin pans, to make darling little puffs for a tea party. Try to use fresh yeast if possible, but if you can't find it, 8 ml of active dried yeast (not instant) will be fine.

200 ml lukewarm milk
5 ml castor sugar
5 ml salt
25 g (half a cube) fresh yeast, crumbled
1 egg
60 ml sunflower oil
560 ml (315 g) cake flour, sifted

Combine the milk, sugar and salt in a large bowl. Stir in the yeast and leave to stand for a few minutes. Add the egg, oil and then the flour; beat well for 1 minute. Cover the bowl and leave to rise in a warm place for about 1 hour.

Preheat the oven to 200 °C. Grease a regular size, 12-cup muffin pan very well.

Beat the batter again, then drop spoonfuls into the muffin pan cups; the dough will be a bit sticky, so you may have to use two spoons. (Each cup should be about two-thirds full.) Leave to rise again until just protruding above the tops of the cups.

Bake for 12–15 minutes until the puffs are golden-brown, then turn out of the pan onto a wire rack to cool.

Makes 12

Do your little bit of good where you are. It is those little bits of good put together that overwhelm the world.

ARCHBISHOP DESMOND TUTU

Pull up a chair. Take a taste.
Come join us. Life is so endlessly delicious.

RUTH REICHL

Food is, of course, an integral part of any celebration, wherever you are in the world. And I don't only mean the so-called traditional celebrations such as Christmas, Passover, Eid or Diwali, but those celebrations that are more personal to families and communities: the weddings, births, farewells and welcomes; the brightly coloured grace notes in the pattern of our days.

When I look back, I can remember lots of parties and celebrations, sometimes at our home, with my mother at the helm, preparing plates and plates of food, as well as flowers and decorations, sometimes at the homes of family and friends. They were not necessarily elaborate or expensive – I think we all had fairly simple tastes so the familiar and traditional recipes were always the most welcome. As we grow older we start to create our own memories and build celebrations around those, too – without losing the ones of the past.

The recipes in this section of the book are part of the tapestry of my life – puddings and cakes and cookies that were at the heart of these special times. I cannot make them without feeling a touch of nostalgia for what are now mostly just memories – but they are good memories, and deserve to be treasured.

And celebrating doesn't need to be expensive, particularly time-consuming or exhausting – most people I know are happier with a glass of sparkling wine and a slice of delicious chocolate cake for a birthday party than an esoteric five-course menu that has taken all day to prepare! What matters most is the love, friendship and happiness that is shared. The food is merely the icing on the cake, but it needs to be really good icing!

Over the Rainbow Birthday Cake

Bright and colourful, this is the perfect cake for a perfect day. It is wonderfully old-fashioned with three rainbow layers – a party on a plate! Candles are the best decoration, or little colourful flags bearing messages and good wishes. Bake this cake and give it with love for wishes to come true.

230 g butter, softened
500 ml (420 g) castor sugar
4 eggs
5 ml vanilla extract
750 ml (420 g) cake flour
20 ml baking powder
3 ml salt
250 ml milk
pink food colouring
45 ml cocoa powder
30 ml boiling water

CREAMY VANILLA ICING
175 g softened butter
375 ml (195 g) icing sugar, sifted
5 ml vanilla extract

A birthday is just the first day of another 365-day journey around the sun. Enjoy the trip.

ANON

Preheat the oven to 180 °C. Grease 3 x 20-cm cake pans very well.

In a large mixing bowl, cream the butter and castor sugar together until light and fluffy. Add the eggs one at a time, followed by the vanilla, and beat well. Sift together the flour, baking powder and salt, then add to the butter mixture, alternately with the milk in three or four parts. (The batter should be thick and smooth.)

Divide the batter into 3 batches. To one batch, add a little pink food colouring to create the desired shade. Combine the cocoa and boiling water and add to the second batch, beating well. Leave the third batch plain vanilla. Transfer the different batters to the 3 cake pans and bake for about 25 minutes, until the cakes are risen and a tester comes out clean. Turn out onto a wire rack and leave to cool. Ice with Creamy vanilla icing and decorate as desired.

To make the icing, add the butter to a bowl and gradually beat in the icing sugar until thick and fluffy. Stir in the vanilla.

Serves 10–12

Lemon Cloud Cake

This is another of my Mom's recipes – I sometimes think she should be writing this book. The cake really lives up to its name: so light and ethereal in texture. It seems to say 'celebration'; perfect for a birthday tea, or even as a light dessert after a special dinner. Two things to note; it should be eaten the day it is made, and try to use homemade lemon curd (see opposite). The synthetic gloop they sell in shops bears little resemblance to the real thing!

3 eggs, separated
200 ml (170 g) castor sugar
juice and grated rind of 1 lemon
125 ml (60 g) cornflour
icing sugar to dust
extra lemon rind, finely grated (optional)
fresh cream to serve

FILLING
250 ml fresh cream
125 ml lemon curd

Preheat the oven to 180 °C. Grease well and line 2 x 23-cm cake pans with baking paper.

Using an electric beater, beat the egg yolks with the castor sugar and lemon rind and juice until very thick and pale. Gently fold in the cornflour with a metal spoon. Whisk the egg whites until they form stiff peaks, but are not dry, then fold into the lemon mixture. Pour into the prepared cake pans. Bake for about 25 minutes, until well risen and golden. (Don't worry if the tops crack, they're supposed to!) Leave to cool in the pans for 5 minutes, then turn out onto wire racks.

To make the filling, whip the cream to soft peaks, then gently fold in the lemon curd. Fill the cake layers with this mixture and dust the top with icing sugar and more lemon zest if you like. Serve very fresh, with more cream.

Serves 8–10

My Mom's Delicious Lemon Curd

juice and finely grated rind of 2 lemons	250 ml (210 g) castor sugar
55 g butter	2 eggs

In a heavy-bottomed saucepan, combine the lemon juice and rind with the butter and sugar. Heat gently until the butter has melted. Beat the eggs well, then stir into the lemon mixture. Cook very gently, stirring constantly, until the mixture is thick and creamy. Remove from the heat and leave to cool. Bottle the curd in small, sterilised jars and keep refrigerated.

Makes ±300 ml

Time for a little something!

WINNIE THE POOH

Queen Anne's Cake with Orange-Brandy Icing

Carrot cake always seems to be popular, but it can be a bit heavy and dry – not this cake, though. The recipe is based on one I found in Camille Glenn's book The Heritage of Southern Cooking*, although I have tweaked it a bit over the years. It's a big, beautiful cake that looks (and tastes spectacular) for a special occasion or gathering. When I originally created the icing I used orange liqueur, such as Cointreau, but it has become so expensive that I cheat with orange juice and brandy instead!*

250 g butter, softened
500 ml (420 g) castor sugar
4 eggs, separated
500 ml peeled and finely grated carrots
250 ml (280 g) cake flour
10 ml ground cinnamon
5 ml ground ginger
5 ml baking powder
5 ml salt
5 ml vanilla extract

ORANGE-BRANDY ICING
30 ml fresh orange juice
finely grated zest of half an orange
30 ml brandy
125 g butter, softened
625 ml (425 g) icing sugar
30 ml sour cream

*Vegetables are a must on a diet.
I suggest carrot cake, zucchini bread and pumpkin pie.*

JIM DAVIS – THE CREATOR OF GARFIELD

le gâteau aux carottes

Preheat the oven to 180 °C. Grease a large (25 cm) tube or bundt cake pan very well.

Cream the butter and castor sugar very well. Beat in the egg yolks until the mixture is smooth and creamy like mayonnaise. Stir in the carrots. Sift together the flour and remaining dry ingredients, then fold into the carrot mixture. Stir in the vanilla. Beat the egg whites in a glass bowl until they are stiff, but not dry or grainy. Fold them lightly into the batter. Spoon the mixture into the prepared pan and bake for approximately 35 minutes, until risen and a tester comes out clean. Leave the cake to cool for at least 20 minutes in the pan before turning out carefully onto a wire rack to cool completely.

To make the icing, mix together the orange juice, orange zest and brandy. In a bowl, cream together the butter, icing sugar and orange-brandy mixture to form a soft, smooth icing. Stir in the sour cream. (If the mixture is too liquid, add a little more icing sugar.) Spread generously over the top and sides of the cold cake. Serve as soon as possible; although the cake may be stored in the fridge, in a sealed container, for a couple of days.

Serves at least 10–12

The Best Cheesecake!

This is a fridge cheesecake, with no baking involved apart from the biscuit crust. Perhaps I am taking a chance calling it 'the best', but I honestly don't know of a more delicious and creamy version of this treat! (I find some baked cheesecakes can be a bit heavy in the mouth.) This was an often-asked for dessert all through my childhood – and I remember how proud I was when, aged about twelve, I first made it by myself, for my mom's dinner party guests. Please use the creamiest cream cheese you can find – not a low-fat option!

Only from the heart can you touch the sky.

RUMI

60 g butter
250 ml (120 g) digestive biscuit crumbs
15 ml gelatine powder
60 ml cold water
250 g tub plain cream cheese
385 g can condensed milk
15 ml lemon juice
250 ml fresh cream, whipped
thin ribbons lemon zest to decorate

Preheat the oven to 180 °C. Grease a deep 23-cm pie dish well.

First make the crust; melt the butter and stir in the biscuit crumbs. Press into the prepared pie dish, and bake for 8–10 minutes, until just turning golden-brown. Leave the crust to cool.

Soak the gelatine in the cold water for 10 minutes, then dissolve over a bowl of boiling water. In a large bowl, beat together the cream cheese, condensed milk and lemon juice. Stir in the gelatine, then fold in the whipped cream. Pour over the cooled biscuit crust.

This cheesecake looks charming if decorated with thin ribbons of lemon zest, and it should be served with extra cream! Keep refrigerated until serving time.

Serves 8

Living a Sweet Life

Like most of us, I started dreaming early – of what I would be, and what I wanted from life. Way back then, interestingly, I already thought of writing cookbooks, with my own little illustrations, and generally following my own creative path. Naturally, when I left school I was encouraged to do something a little more sensible, such as studying to be a secretary. Looking back, that was not exactly the best fit for me!

As the years went by, I did do a number of different things, and explored several avenues, including writing and design, which was my chief source of income for a long time. I even did a little professional baking, although I never went to culinary school, which was another plan I put on hold. I often felt a little scattered, as though all the bits of my life and work were never going to make any kind of a cohesive whole.

Then I remembered a fairy story I had loved as a child, about a beautiful but penniless, girl in the village, who was invited to a glittering ball. Needless to say she could not afford a beautiful dress, but she remembered that in a chest in the attic were many pieces of fabric, all different colours and patterns and textures. Being good with her needle, she set to and created a patchwork dress for herself, like a rainbow. To cut a long story short, she was the most beautiful sight at the ball, and won the prince's heart of course! But, like all good fairy stories, there was a deeper meaning – that sometimes what

seems like odds and ends, a scrapbag of life's experiences without much value, can turn out to be the greatest treasure of all.

So, a few years ago, when I realised that I had wandered off my path and lost a part of myself (sound familiar?), I decided to slow down and focus on getting back to where I had wanted to be; 'a path with heart', as it has been so beautifully described. It's an ongoing process, of course, but even this book is a part of that – the book I dreamed of writing so long ago. I do believe that the dreams and wishes we have before the world has too great a grip on us, and our hearts are still open, are the true and lovely ones.

Perhaps loving something is the only basis there is for making your life your own.

ALICE KOLLER

Saint Nicholas Cake

This is another 'old' recipe – from the 1940s, I believe. It's a slightly different take on a traditional fruitcake, and even people who aren't big fans of fruitcake usually seem to like it. (The chocolate chips are optional, but they do add an interesting taste dimension.) The recipe makes one large or two small loaves – I like to bake two loaves, using foil loaf pans, and then wrap one up in cellophane and finish it off with a great big gingham bow as a delicious gift!

- 3 eggs
- 200 ml (170 g) castor sugar
- 5 ml vanilla extract
- 375 ml (210 g) cake flour
- 5 ml baking powder
- 3 ml salt
- 250 g stoned dates, finely chopped
- 75 g glace cherries, chopped
- 30 ml cake flour
- 75 g pecan nuts, roughly chopped
- 75 g dark chocolate chips (optional)
- brandy or apple juice

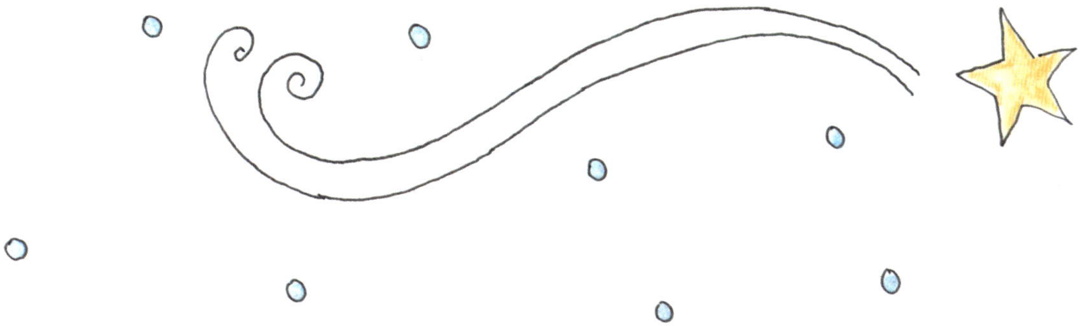

Preheat the oven to 150 °C. Grease 1 large or 2 small loaf pans very well.

Using an electric mixer if possible, beat the eggs, sugar and vanilla together very well, until the mixture is thick and pale. Sift together the 375 ml flour, baking powder and salt, then add to the egg mixture gradually, beating well to form a smooth batter.

Mix the dates and cherries with the 30 ml flour (this stops them from sinking in the cake). Stir the dates, cherries, pecan nuts and chocolate chips (if using) into the batter. Spread the batter evenly in the prepared pan(s).

Stand the pan(s) in a roasting dish half-filled with water on the lower rack of the oven and bake for 90 minutes, or until golden-brown and a tester comes out clean. Leave to cool completely in the pans, then brush with brandy or apple juice before turning out. These loaves are nicest if wrapped in foil and left to mature for a few days before serving.

Makes 1 large or 2 small loaves

All you have to do is look hard enough, and what might seem to be a series of unfortunate events may, in fact be the first steps of a journey …

LEMONY SNICKET

Cathy's Christmas Cake

The world seems to be divided between those who love fruitcake passionately, and those who just can't stand it. I am one of the former, so you can imagine how much I looked forward to the Christmas season and my mom's fruit cake, which she always made some time in early November. (According to tradition, we would all get to stir the mixture, and make a wish!) Then she kept it well wrapped, doused with a weekly dose of brandy, until just before Christmas, when it would be completed with a layer of marzipan, and white fluffy icing that looked just like snow. I always got to add the finishing touches – the little trees and houses and snowmen that made it look just like a holiday wonderland. Sometimes the simplest, and oldest traditions are the best of all!

Christmas is not as much about opening our presents, as opening our hearts.

JANICE MAEDITERE

250 g raisins
250 g currants
250 g sultanas
125 ml brandy
180 g butter, softened
375 ml (300 g) brown sugar

4 eggs
250 ml (140 g) cake flour
250 ml (140 g) self-raising flour
5 ml salt
5 ml mixed spice

Wash the raisins, currants and sultanas, then place in a large bowl. Pour over the brandy and leave to soak overnight.

Preheat the oven to 160 °C. Grease a deep, 22-cm cake pan very well and line the base with baking paper.

Cream the butter and sugar, then beat in the eggs one at a time. Fold in the two flours, salt and spice. Mix the brandy-soaked fruit into the cake, until the batter is well blended, then spoon into the prepared cake pan, smoothing the top. Bake for approximately 1 hour, then reduce the oven temperature to 150 °C, cover the top of the pan with aluminium foil (shiny side down) and bake for another 90 minutes. Leave in the pan until cold, then turn out and wrap in foil.

Store the cake in an airtight container for several weeks, but each week open the cake and brush the top and sides generously with more brandy or sherry!

Serves 10–12

Mincemeat Cake with Brandy Butter Icing

Another fruit cake – sorry for those non-fruitcake eaters – but this one is a little different, and really easy to make. It makes a great alternative at Christmas and, sometimes, I adapt it a bit by leaving out the icing, warming slices of the cake and serving them as a simplified holiday pudding, with the brandy butter on the side (and cream, of course!). The fruit mincemeat available in jars is actually quite good, but I tend to tart mine up a bit, very simply, by stirring in 30 ml of brandy and 30 ml of fresh orange juice.

Gifts of time and love are surely the basic ingredients of a truly merry Christmas.

PEG BRACKEN

125 g butter, softened
160 g light brown sugar
2 eggs, beaten
225 g fruit mincemeat
60 ml orange juice
375 ml (310 g) cake flour
30 ml baking powder
3 ml salt
3 ml bicarbonate of soda
5 ml mixed spice

BRANDY BUTTER
60 g butter, softened
200 ml (100 g) icing sugar, sifted
30 ml brandy

Preheat the oven to 170 °C. Grease a deep 20-cm round cake pan well, and line the base with baking paper. Beat the butter and light brown sugar together well, until light and fluffy. Gradually beat in the eggs, then stir in the mincemeat and orange juice.

Sift together the flour, baking powder, salt, bicarbonate of soda and mixed spice, and stir into the mincemeat mixture. Beat well, then spoon the batter, which should be fairly thick, into the cake pan. Level the surface. Bake for about 1 hour, until the cake is firm and a tester comes out clean. (Don't worry if there are a few cracks on the surface!) Leave in the pan for 10 minutes, then turn out onto a wire rack to cool completely.

To make the brandy butter, cream together the butter and icing sugar until light and fluffy. Beat in the brandy. Either spread the icing over the top of the cooled cake, or serve it on the side.

Serves 8–10

Blitz Torte

Just beautiful, a party on a plate, light and rich at the same time! This will turn any occasion into a celebration and is really simple to make. (The original recipe comes from the old red Betty Crocker book but I have tweaked it a little.)

125 g butter, softened
200 ml (170 g) castor sugar
5 ml vanilla extract
4 eggs, separated
125 ml (140 g) cake flour
5 ml baking powder
3 ml salt

45 ml milk
250 ml (210 g) castor sugar
125 ml fresh cream
5 ml vanilla extract
250 ml vanilla custard
125 ml (75 g) slivered almonds
30 ml icing sugar (optional)

You just have to get rid of the baggage to be light enough to dance, to sing, to play ...

ANNE LAMOTT

Preheat the oven to 160 °C. Grease 2 x 20-cm round cake pans well.

Cream the butter, 200 ml castor sugar and vanilla together until light and fluffy. Beat in the egg yolks. Sift the flour, baking powder and salt together then mix into the butter mixture. Stir in the milk.

Divide the batter evenly between the pans. Using an electric beater, whisk the egg whites until soft peaks form; then gradually whisk in the 250 ml castor sugar until the meringue mixture is stiff and glossy. Spread half of the meringue over the batter in each pan. Bake for 50–60 minutes until the meringue is pale golden and set. Leave to cool, then remove each cake carefully from its pan.

Just before serving, beat the cream with the vanilla extract and fold into the custard. Place the first cake layer on a serving plate, meringue side up. Spread carefully with the custard mixture. Sprinkle over half of the almonds. Gently place the second cake layer on top, meringue side up, and sprinkle with the remaining almonds. Dust with icing sugar if you like.

Serves 8–10

Honey Bee Cake

There are cakes, and then there are cakes, with a capital C. This is one of the latter in my opinion: buttery golden layers filled with dark chocolate ganache, and not a drop of honey! (The name comes from the striped appearance, which makes one think of a bee.) Pure celebration in a cake, for any day or anyone special. (I like to make it in smaller layer pans, so that the three layers are not too thin. The rum syrup is not essential – it's an idea adapted from professional bakeries, which adds a little depth to the cake's flavour.)

CAKE
560 ml (315g) cake flour
15 ml baking powder
5 ml salt
125 g butter
375 ml (315 g) castor sugar
3 eggs
10 ml vanilla extract
250 ml milk

SYRUP
125 ml (100 g) granulated white sugar
125 ml water
15 ml rum (or brandy or vodka)

CHOCOLATE GANACHE
125 ml fresh cream
250 g dark chocolate, chopped
60 g unsalted butter

A house is not beautiful because of its walls.
A house is beautiful because of its cakes.

RUSSIAN PROVERB

Preheat the oven to 180 °C. Grease 2 or 3 x 20-cm layer pans very well.

To make the cake, sift together the flour, baking powder and salt. Beat the butter and castor sugar together very well, preferably with an electric mixer, until light and fluffy. Add the eggs and vanilla extract gradually, and beat well, until the mixture is well combined. Add the sifted dry ingredients in three additions, alternating with the milk. Divide the batter evenly according to the number of pans. Bake for 30–35 minutes, until the cakes are lightly browned on the edges and a tester comes out clean. Leave to cool in the pans for 20 minutes, then turn out onto a wire rack to cool completely.

If you are making the syrup, combine the sugar and water in a small saucepan, and bring to the boil for at least 10 minutes (stirring occasionally), then remove from the heat. Stir in the rum, and leave to cool completely.

For the ganache, warm the cream gently in a heavy-bottomed saucepan but do not allow to boil. Place the chocolate and butter in a glass bowl, and set the bowl over a pan of gently simmering water. Pour the warm cream over the chocolate and stir until the chocolate and butter have melted, and the mixture is smooth. Leave to cool slightly (the ganache should be spreadable, but not too thick).

To assemble the cake, brush a little of the syrup (if using) over each layer. Fill the cake layers with the chocolate ganache and also spread over the top of the cake. Serve at once, or refrigerate for no more than two days. (Bring back to room temperature before serving, otherwise the chocolate will be too hard.)

Serves 8–10

Creating the Moment ...

I truly believe that one of the greatest gifts we have to bring to the world (and ourselves) is creativity. And I also believe that it is fresh and unique to every single one of us. If I make a birthday cake, it will not look like yours, or taste like yours, even if we follow the same recipe. Everything reflects a little of the soul of its creator.

And maybe it's the everyday creations that are the best of all. After all, not all of us are going to paint magnificent pictures, or play music on a concert stage, but we can all bake and cook, and create a little magic on the plate for those we love.

I was lucky to have a mother and other adults around me who supported and nurtured my creativity when I was little, in the kitchen and out. Some of us are not given this kind of support, but the good news is we can all tap into it again, any time, and at any age. It just takes a little bit of courage, to say 'yes', to your life and your individuality. So create something delicious in your kitchen today, as a starting point – and you will be on the way to creating a life that honours itself.

Creativity is a way of living life, no matter our vocation, or how we earn our living.

MADELEINE L'ENGLE

Irish Chocolate Cake

No prizes for guessing the secret ingredient in this dark, lush chocolate cake – it's that wonderful Irish nectar, Guinness. (You can use milk stout instead.) This recipe was, like so many others in this book, given to me by a friend in London. She was actually Indian, which just goes to show how recipes travel and make friends wherever they go! Meena told me she always served the cake plain, with some whipped cream on the side, as she didn't feel it needed lots of sweet icing – and I agree with her on that.

- 125 ml (75 g) raisins
- 125 ml Guinness
- 60 ml cocoa powder
- 125 ml boiling water
- 125 g butter, softened
- 250 ml (210 g) castor sugar
- 3 eggs, separated
- 200 ml (110 g) cake flour
- 5 ml baking powder
- 3 ml salt
- 125 ml (50 g) ground almonds

Preheat the oven to 160 °C. Grease a fairly deep 20-cm round springform pan well.

A few hours before you plan to make the cake, place the raisins in a small bowl, pour over the Guinness and leave to soak. Mix the cocoa with boiling water in another bowl, stir until the mixture is smooth, then leave to cool.

Cream together the butter and sugar until light and fluffy. Stir in the egg yolks, one at a time. Sift together the flour, baking powder, salt and almonds, then combine with the butter mixture until creamy and smooth. Add the raisins and Guinness, and beat again well. Whisk the egg whites until stiff but not dry; then gently fold them into the batter, taking care not to overbeat. Pour the batter into the prepared pan and bake for approximately 35–40 minutes, or until a tester comes out clean. Leave to cool on a wire rack for 30 minutes before removing from the pan. Serve as fresh as possible.

Serves 8–10

The way to 'get there' is to 'be there'.
Just be where you choose to go. It's that simple!

NEALE DONALD WALSCH

Elvis's Birthday Cake

The music of Elvis Presley formed part of the soundtrack of my life when I was growing up in the '60s and '70s. I was in my last year at school when he died; I remember walking into the classroom that day to find some of my friends in tears, and their mothers too. About eight years ago I was given a wonderful American cookbook all about birthday cakes, and there was a special birthday cake for Elvis (his birthday is 8 January, in case you were wondering). It was created by a baker and cookbook author, Maria Sanchez, after she read that peanut butter and banana was Elvis's favourite sandwich filling. I have changed her recipe quite a bit, but the general theme is there, and I love making it for people who enjoy his music. It's a sweet tribute to a brilliant talent lost too soon. (You can use smooth or chunky peanut butter in the cake, whichever you prefer.)

90 g butter, softened
80 ml peanut butter
375 ml (315 g) castor sugar
2 eggs
500 ml (280 g) cake flour
15 ml baking powder
5 ml salt
60 ml cocoa powder
250 ml buttermilk
375 ml cream
30 ml granulated white sugar
2 medium bananas

"Love Me Tender..."

It was like he came along and whispered some dream in everyone's ear, and somehow we all dreamed it ...

BRUCE SPRINGSTEEN (ABOUT ELVIS)

Preheat the oven to 180 °C. Grease 2 x 23-cm round cake pans well.

Cream together the butter, peanut butter and castor sugar until light and fluffy. Stir in the eggs, one at a time. Sift together the flour, baking powder, salt and cocoa, then beat into the butter mixture. Stir in the buttermilk and beat well.

Divide the batter evenly between the pans and bake for 20–25 minutes, until a tester comes out clean. Leave to cool briefly in the pans, then turn out onto a wire rack, to cool completely.

Whip the cream with the granulated white sugar until stiff. Peel the bananas, and slice them fairly thinly. Place one of the cake layers on a serving plate, and spread with half the cream. Arrange half the banana slices on top of this. Cover with the second cake layer, then top with the remaining cream and banana. (It looks even prettier if you dust the top with a little cocoa.) Refrigerate the cake for 1–2 hours before serving.

Serves 8–10

Caramel Almond Bars

Do people still go on picnics? Probably not as much as they used to, which is a pity but also understandable given the issue of safety. We had lots of picnics when I was growing up – in our own garden, in parks, on the beach or just by the side of the road when travelling somewhere. There was always coffee in a flask to drink, made with condensed milk, and something sweet and sticky to eat, such as these caramel almond bars. And somehow these picnics always felt like a celebration, even if it was just of being alive and out in the sunshine, going somewhere ...

- 125 g butter, softened
- 125 ml (105 g) castor sugar
- 250 ml (140 g) cake flour, sifted
- 2 eggs
- 250 ml (200 g) light brown sugar
- 5 ml vanilla extract
- 5 ml baking powder
- 3 ml salt
- 250 ml (150 g) flaked almonds
- 30 ml cake flour

Preheat the oven to 180 °C. Grease an 18 x 28 cm baking pan very well.

Mix the butter, castor sugar and 250 ml flour together, to form a soft dough. Press evenly and thinly over the base of the prepared pan and bake for 10 minutes, until just set. Leave to cool briefly.

For the topping, beat the eggs and light brown sugar together well. Stir in the vanilla extract, baking powder, salt, almonds and 30 ml flour. Spread this mixture over the cooled base, and return to the oven for another 25 minutes, or until the topping is golden-brown. Leave to cool slightly in the pan, then cut into bars.

Makes ±20 bars

When you're travelling, you create yourself right there and then. People don't hold your past against you. No yesterdays on the road.

WILLIAM LEAST HEAT MOON

Chocolate Chip Shortbread Fans

My mother loves shortbread, and she has always been particularly fond of the boxes of shortbread wedges filled with chocolate chips, which are imported from Scotland. Unfortunately, as one now has to take out a bank loan to afford them, I had to make a plan – and this recipe is the result. (I think this shortbread tastes a lot better, anyway!) Boxes of these make a really wonderful gift – for some reason I always pack them in pink gift boxes tied up with pink and white polka dot ribbon, a little over the top perhaps, but fun!

125 g unsalted butter, softened
60 ml (50 g) castor sugar
310 ml (175 g) cake flour
60 ml (30 g) cornflour
a pinch of salt
125 ml (100 g) chocolate chips

It is the sweet, simple things of life which are the real ones, after all.

LAURA INGALLS WILDER

Preheat the oven to 170 °C. Grease a shallow 20-cm cake pan well.

Cream the butter and sugar together until light and creamy. Sift together the cake flour, cornflour and salt, then mix into the butter mixture. Add the chocolate chips and stir well to make a fairly firm but manageable dough. Press the dough evenly into the prepared pan, and prick well with a fork. Mark the round into 8–10 wedges.

Bake for 40–45 minutes until a very pale golden-brown (don't allow the shortbread to become too dark). Cut into wedges while still warm, then leave to cool in the pan on a wire rack. Shortbread does keep well in a tin, but the question never seems to arise!

Makes 8–10 wedges

Coffee-Glazed Cream Puffs

I have lovely childhood memories of my mom making these puffs – for parties and other occasions – filling them with whipped cream and glazing them with dark chocolate. My version is slightly different as I use a creamy, coffee-flavoured glaze instead. They can be served individually on plates, of course, but a really special presentation is to pile them in a pyramid on a cake plate and drizzle the sauce over them. Add candles for a unique birthday cake!

CREAM PUFFS

250 ml water
90 g unsalted butter
3 ml salt
250 ml (140 g) cake flour
4 eggs, room temperature
500 ml whipping cream

COFFEE GLAZE

45 ml instant coffee granules
250 ml (210 g) castor sugar
250 ml water
125 ml cream

I saw food as something beautiful to be shared with people, instead of as a thrice-daily necessity.

MFK FISHER

Preheat the oven to 200 °C. Line a large baking sheet with baking paper.

In a medium saucepan, combine the water, butter and salt; then bring to the boil until the butter has melted. Add the flour all at once, beating hard to form a thick paste that comes away from the sides of the pan. Remove from the heat and leave to cool briefly. Add the eggs, one at a time (you may not need the last egg) to form a smooth, shiny dough. Use a tablespoon to make mounds of dough on the prepared baking sheet. (You should have about 24.)

Bake the puffs for 20–25 minutes until golden-brown. Turn off the heat. Remove the puffs from oven, make a small slit in the side of each then return them to oven for 5 minutes. Leave to cool completely. Whip the cream until stiff then use it to fill the puffs – just before serving.

To make the glaze, in a heavy-bottomed saucepan bring the coffee, sugar and water to the boil until a thick syrup is formed. Remove from the heat and leave to cool to lukewarm before stirring in the cream. Glaze the cream-filled puffs with this mixture just before serving.

Makes ±24

Toffee-Chocolate Shortbread Squares

A favourite of my dear Terry – always made at his request for birthdays and other special occasions – even though he always said eating so many of them would be his downfall! They are undoubtedly rich, but sometimes you just have to throw caution to the wind and enjoy!

BASE	FILLING AND TOPPING
250 ml (140 g cake flour	65 g butter
60 ml (50 g) castor sugar	60 ml golden syrup
3 ml salt	125 ml (100 g) light brown sugar
125 g butter, cubed	385 g can condensed milk
	5 ml vanilla essence
	125 g milk chocolate

A single rose can be my garden.
A single friend my world.

LEO BUSCAGLIA

Preheat the oven to 160 °C. Grease a 23-cm square baking pan very well.

To make the base, combine the flour, castor sugar and salt, then rub in the butter to form a dough. Press the dough evenly over the base of the prepared pan. Bake for 15 minutes until just pale golden. Leave to cool briefly.

For the filling, mix the butter, syrup, light brown sugar and condensed milk in a saucepan, stirring all the time until the sugar has dissolved and the mixture has slightly thickened. Remove from the heat and stir in the vanilla. Pour the mixture over the cooled pastry base and spread it evenly. Leave to cool. Melt the chocolate by heating it in a bowl over a pan of simmering water, or in a microwave. Spread the chocolate evenly over the filling. Leave to cool completely before cutting into squares.

Makes 16

Marie's Spice Pudding

This, to me, will always be the 'other' Christmas pudding. During my childhood, we usually spent Christmas Day with my aunt and uncle and four cousins. My mom always made a traditional Christmas pudding with dried fruit, but as my cousins weren't too keen on that, Aunty Marie also made her version of this traditional Afrikaans recipe, which had been handed down to her as a girl on a farm in what was then the Northern Transvaal. (She always included many 5c- and 10c-pieces, so that whoever found them could make a wish!)

125 g butter, softened
250 ml (200 g) light brown sugar
1 egg
5 ml ground ginger
5 ml bicarbonate of soda
30 ml apricot jam

375 ml (210 g) cake flour
8 ml baking powder
125 ml milk

SYRUP
250 ml (200 g) light brown sugar
500 ml boiling water

It has been said many times that our lives are gifts from God – Christmas is the perfect day to remember that …

SARAH BAN BREATHNACH

Preheat the oven to 180 °C. Grease a rectangular baking dish well.

Cream the butter and light brown sugar together well. Add the egg, ginger, bicarbonate of soda and apricot jam. Sift the flour and baking powder together, then stir into the butter mixture. Add the milk – just enough to give the dough a soft, dropping consistency.

Mix the syrup ingredients, then pour it into the base of the prepared baking dish. Spoon the batter over the syrup.

Bake for approximately 1 hour (covered for the first 10 minutes), or until the pudding is golden-brown and the sauce is thick. Serve piping hot, with lots of custard or thick cream.

Serves 4–6

Granadilla Meringue Pie

We had a large granadilla vine in the garden of my childhood home, and I loved picking the knobbly little purple fruit, cutting them in half and scooping out the delicious pulp with a teaspoon. They're also known as passion fruit – what a wonderful name! This pie, a delightful alternative to the more usual lemon meringue pie, also tends to incite a certain amount of passion, and makes a great dessert for any special occasion of the heart.

BISCUIT CRUST

180 g digestive, Tennis or Marie biscuits, crushed
30 ml castor sugar
90 g melted butter

FILLING

110 g can granadilla pulp
385 g can condensed milk
2 extra large eggs, separated
200 ml (170 g) castor sugar

First prepare the biscuit crust. Preheat the oven to 180 °C. Grease a 23-cm pie dish well. Combine the crushed biscuits with the 30 ml castor sugar and melted butter. Press into the dish and bake for approximately 8 minutes.

To make the filling, preheat the oven to 160 °C. Place the granadilla pulp in a mixing bowl, then stir in the condensed milk and beat in the egg yolks until thoroughly combined. Spread the granadilla mixture over the prepared biscuit crust. To make the meringue, in a glass bowl beat the egg whites until frothy, then gradually beat in the 200 ml castor sugar until the mixture is stiff but not dry. Using a spatula or large spoon, carefully spread the meringue over the pie filling, ensuring that it is completely covered to the edges.

Bake the pie for around 45–50 minutes, or until the meringue topping is set and a pale golden shade at the tips. Leave to cool completely, then refrigerate until serving.

Meringue pies are best eaten within 1–2 days, otherwise the meringue tends to soften and become syrupy.

Serves 6–8

There is no passion to be found in playing small – in settling for a life that is less than the one you are capable of living.

NELSON MANDELA

Lemon Syllabub Trifle with Strawberries

There was a time when no celebration was complete without a large trifle, made with custard, jelly, brightly coloured fruit and, of course, a hefty dose of sherry. This is a much older recipe – although it still has the sherry! – that dates, in part, back to Victorian times. The syllabub is an even older treat, and can be served as a dessert in its own right. The trifle must be started the day before you plan to serve it, and does take some time to make, but I think it's worth it. (If you prefer, you can use little raspberries instead of strawberries – and please bear in mind that this is a fairly grown-up dessert, given the quantity of alcohol involved!) A large, deep and beautiful glass bowl is a must – I use a wonderful one I bought for 59c at a church fête!

TRIFLE	SYLLABUB
175 g Boudoir biscuits (or sliced sponge cake)	juice and zest of 2 small lemons
125 ml cream sherry or Marsala	80 ml sweet white wine
250 g sliced strawberries	30 ml brandy
500 ml vanilla custard	60 ml (50 g) castor sugar
extra strawberries to garnish	500 ml whipping cream

I cook with wine. Sometimes
I even add it to the food.

WC FIELDS

The day before you plan to serve the trifle, arrange half the biscuits or cake in a large, deep glass bowl, with a capacity of at least 1.1 litres. Sprinkle over half the sherry or Marsala, then top with the remaining biscuits or cake, followed by the rest of the sherry. Leave to stand in a cool place for at least 12 hours, or overnight.

To make the syllabub, place the lemon juice and zest in a bowl, with the wine, brandy and sugar. Stir until the sugar has dissolved. Cover and leave overnight.

The next day, complete the syllabub first. Strain the lemon mixture into a large bowl. Gradually pour in the cream, stirring all the time. Using a hand whisk or rotary beater, whisk the mixture until it forms soft peaks. (This can take up to 10 minutes and must be done slowly and carefully so as not to overbeat, which results in an unusable mixture. For this reason an electric mixer is unsuitable.)

To assemble the trifle, arrange the strawberries on top of the biscuit mixture in the bowl. Spoon the custard over the strawberries, then top with the lemon syllabub, swirling it decoratively. Garnish with extra strawberries, or lemon zest if you like, then chill for 2 hours before serving.

Serves 8–10

Caramel Pavlova with Raspberries and Cream

When I was young, my favourite birthday dessert was meringue with cream and chocolate sauce – and sometimes ice cream as well! Simple, sweet tastes that are still good. This takes the whole concept a little bit further – and I think the raspberry sauce makes a colourful and tasty addition. (You could also use chocolate or caramel sauce, if you prefer.) This is just such a delicious, yet elegant dessert, it is never out of place. The brown sugar gives the Pavlova its delicate caramel flavour; sift it first to ensure it is free of lumps, or give it a brief whizz in a food processor.

RASPBERRY SAUCE

250 g raspberries (or small, cleaned strawberries)
60 ml (50 g) castor sugar
30 ml brandy (optional)
5 ml vanilla extract

PAVLOVA

2 egg whites, room temperature
3 ml cream of tartar
125 ml (100 g) light brown sugar
250 ml whipping cream

Cooking is like love. It should be entered into with abandon, or not at all.

HARRIET VAN HORNE

Make the raspberry sauce first. Combine the raspberries, castor sugar, brandy and vanilla in a heavy-bottomed saucepan, and simmer until the berries are soft, making sure the mixture does not become dry. (You can purée the sauce with a handheld stick blender, but I prefer it a little chunky.) Remove from the heat, leave to cool, then store in a glass jar; the sauce will keep in the fridge for 1 week to 10 days.

For the Pavlova, preheat the oven to 130 °C. Line a large baking sheet with baking paper and draw a circle about 23 cm in diameter on the paper. Put the egg whites and cream of tartar in a metal or glass bowl, and whisk, preferably with an electric whisk. When the whites form soft peaks, start whisking in the sugar, 15 ml at a time. The meringue is ready when it forms stiff peaks. Spread the meringue to fit in the circle on the baking paper, then build up the sides using a metal spoon, so that you end up with what looks like a meringue pie case.

Bake for 90–120 minutes, until the Pavlova is firm and crisp. Turn off the heat and leave it in the oven for another 30 minutes. Remove and leave to cool completely. Whip the cream and use it to fill the Pavlova just before serving; drizzle with the raspberry sauce. It's best to eat this on the day it is made, as meringue tends to go soft and sticky quite quickly.

Serves 6

Spiced Chicken Puffs

I love making Indian food almost as much as I love baking – and this recipe is an excellent way to combine the two. I first tasted these in an Indian restaurant in London, and although mine are probably not very authentic, they make a wonderful snack or side dish with a curry meal. They are particularly good served with a raita, made by combining thick, creamy yoghurt with grated cucumber, a little crushed garlic, salt and ground cumin.

310 ml (175 g) cake flour	250 g shredded, cooked chicken (no skin)
10 ml baking powder	5 ml minced garlic
5 ml salt	half a small onion, finely chopped
5 ml garam masala	5 ml minced chilli (optional)
2 eggs	30 ml chopped fresh coriander
125 ml plain yoghurt	sunflower oil for frying

Sift together the flour, baking powder, salt and garam masala into a bowl. Beat the eggs and yoghurt together then add to the flour mixture, along with the chicken, garlic, onion, chilli and coriander. Beat until a batter is formed. Heat about 1 cm of oil in a wide saucepan, and fry tablespoons of the mixture, 4 or 5 at a time, until set and golden on both sides. Drain on paper towel and serve warm, if possible.

Makes ±15

Take up one idea. Make that one idea your life – think of it, dream of it, live on that idea.

SWAMI VIVEKANANDA

Cheese and Mustard Gougère

A simple yet perfect start to any celebration – with a little French style! Choux pastry, as I've mentioned before, must be the most rewarding pastry to make; from a pan of thick yellow batter comes something light as air, golden-brown and delicious! The original recipe for gougère uses Gruyère cheese, but I prefer Cheddar and a little Parmesan. Serve the gougère warm, cut into small wedges, with glasses of cold white wine (or champagne!).

- 250 ml water
- 90 g unsalted butter
- 3 ml salt
- 250 ml (140 g) cake flour
- 4 eggs at room temperature
- 30 ml prepared Dijon mustard
- 60 g Cheddar cheese, cut into tiny cubes
- 45 ml grated Parmesan cheese
- paprika to taste

There's a time for departure, even when there's no certain place to go.

TENNESSEE WILLIAMS

Preheat the oven to 220 °C. Line a baking sheet with baking paper; then draw a circle with a 21-cm diameter on the sheet.

In a medium saucepan, bring the water, butter and salt to the boil, stirring until the butter has completely melted. Add all the flour, beating until the mixture forms a thick, smooth paste that comes away from the sides of the pan. Remove from the heat and leave to cool briefly.

Beat in the eggs, one at a time. The dough should be smooth and shiny. (You may not always need the last egg.) Stir in the mustard, cheese and 15 ml of the Parmesan. Using 2 spoons, form a circle on the paper, following the circle outline. The completed circle should be 21 cm in diameter, ±6 cm wide, and 3 cm high. (You can use a piping bag if you prefer.) Sprinkle with the remaining Parmesan and some paprika.

Put the gougère in the oven, reduce the temperature to 200 °C and bake for 25–30 minutes until risen and golden-brown. Turn the oven off and leave the gougère in for another 15 minutes. Leave to cool briefly on a wire rack, then serve in slices.

Serves 6–8

et voila...!

Sweet and Simple

The ordinary arts we practice every day at home are of more importance to the soul than their simplicity might suggest ...

THOMAS MOORE

When I told several of my friends that I was writing a baking book they were all supportive and enthusiastic – bless their hearts! However, almost all of them had a similar query, 'Will the recipes be simple and easy to prepare; not those with 17 ingredients, most of which you don't have to hand, and where actually making the thing takes the better part of the day?'

I like to think that the majority of the recipes in this book are both user-friendly and accessible for most people and budgets. When I was growing up and my mom taught me to bake and cook, we were never overly extravagant in terms of ingredients or the time needed to make something. Of course, there are occasions that call for pushing the boat out a bit – those really special celebrations where you don't mind using good chocolate or nine eggs, but in general, most of us just want to make easy, tasty and simple things that don't cause unnecessary expense (or total exhaustion!).

And while it's a fact that many of us are both cash-strapped and short of time these days, there is also a more positive way of looking at these things, in that people are often consciously looking for simpler and more meaningful ways of living their lives every day – and reflecting those in the choices they make.

So, the recipes in this section of the book are particularly geared to those who want simplicity and deliciousness, all rolled into one! And obviously they are suitable for people who are new to baking, or cooking in general – and for introducing children to the joys of baking.

Cinnamon Breakfast Doughnuts

These aren't 'proper' ring-shaped doughnuts made with yeast, but pretty tasty all the same, and quicker to prepare. My mom sprinkles them with sugar and cinnamon, but I prefer them sweet and glazed. A lovely breakfast or brunch treat with coffee, on a miserably grey day!

500 ml (280 g) cake flour
60 ml (50 g) castor sugar
15 ml baking powder
5 ml salt
5 ml cinnamon
60 ml oil
200 ml milk
1 egg
sunflower oil for frying

GLAZE
250 ml (130 g) icing sugar
boiling water
dash of lemon juice (optional)
5 ml cinnamon (optional)

Mix together the flour, castor sugar, baking powder, salt and cinnamon. In a smaller bowl, beat together the oil, milk and egg. Stir into the dry ingredients, then mix well to form a thick batter. In a pan, heat about 5 cm of sunflower oil and drop large teaspoonfuls of the batter into the hot oil, turning frequently, for about 3 minutes until golden-brown. Drain on paper towel, then dip into the glaze while still warm.

For the glaze, put the icing sugar in a bowl and gradually add enough boiling water to make a fairly thin glaze. You can add a little lemon juice or cinnamon, if you like. Eat as fresh as possible!

Makes 20–25 small doughnuts

Be a rainbow in someone else's cloud

MAYA ANGELOU

Good Morning Banana Bread

Banana bread, sliced and thickly spread with butter, has to be one of life's simplest and most delicious pleasures. It was a staple of the tea table and lunchbox when I was young, although I always felt really sorry for my mother who is allergic to bananas, and so never tasted the delicious loaves she made! This recipe expands a little on the original idea, with the pecans and coconuts – and the aroma during baking is indescribably delicious. The recipe makes two medium-sized loaves, which is not exactly a hardship, since one of them, wrapped up in brown paper and tied with a gingham ribbon, makes the sweetest gift for a friend.

560 ml (315 g) cake flour
5 ml bicarbonate of soda
5 ml baking powder
3 ml salt
125 ml (40 g) desiccated coconut
125 ml (100 g) light brown sugar
250 ml (210 g) castor sugar
2 extra large eggs
5 ml vanilla extract
125 ml sunflower oil
3–4 ripe bananas, peeled and well mashed
125 ml (75 g) chopped pecan nuts

Preheat the oven to 180 °C. Grease two 20 x 10-cm loaf pans very well.

In a large bowl, sift together the flour, bicarbonate of soda, baking powder and salt. Stir in the coconut, then set aside. Using an electric whisk if possible, in another bowl beat both the sugars, eggs and vanilla together until thick and pale (3–4 minutes). Whisk in the oil until just combined, then add the bananas, stirring well to combine. Add the dry ingredients to the batter gradually, mixing lightly. (Do not over-mix the batter.) Stir in the pecans.

Divide the batter between the two prepared pans. Bake until well risen and golden-brown on top and a tester comes out clean (35–40 minutes). Leave to cool in the pans for 20 minutes, then turn out onto a wire rack. The loaves are best if served on the day they are made, but they can be wrapped and kept in the fridge for 3–4 days.

Makes 2 medium loaves

Kentucky Breakfast Pancakes

When I was growing up, breakfast was a simple business – toast or cereal, and a hot drink. The exception was Sundays, when my mom made us something special such as French toast, or omelettes, or pancakes (not the thin pancakes we all love, with cinnamon, sugar and lemon, but the thicker, smaller American-style pancakes). About 15 years ago I bought a wonderful old cookbook in London – The Heritage of Southern Cooking *by Camille Glenn – and in it was a recipe for Kentucky Pancakes. They were quite heavenly, and immediately transported me back to Sunday mornings when I was a child. So, this recipe is really courtesy of Mrs Glenn, although I have modified it over time. It makes a lot of pancakes, too, but somehow they always seem to disappear in record time! I love them served with butter, honey or maple syrup, and crisp rashers of bacon, but there are those who prefer them with cream, fruit, or even ice cream.*

I adore simple pleasures. They are the last refuge of the complex.

OSCAR WILDE

750 ml (350 g) cake flour
10 ml castor sugar
8 ml salt
15 ml baking powder
3 eggs, separated
500 ml milk
90 g butter, melted and cooled
butter and oil for frying

Sift the flour into a large bowl, and stir in the sugar, salt and baking powder. In another bowl, beat the egg yolks well, then add the milk, and beat again. Add the flour mixture and mix thoroughly. Stir in the melted butter. Beat the egg whites until they are stiff, but not dry, then fold them gently into the flour mixture. Leave the batter to stand for 20–30 minutes.

Heat a knob of butter and a few tablespoons of cooking oil in a heavy-bottomed frying pan. Add about 3 tablespoons of batter (per pancake) and fry. (Don't crowd the pan as it's preferable to fry only 2–3 pancakes at a time.) Once the pancakes are golden-brown on one side, turn over with a spatula and brown the other side. Flipping them back and forth toughens them, according to Mrs Glenn!

Serve warm, with the accompaniments of your choice.

Serves 6 (generously)

Friends and other Blessings

Nothing gives me greater pleasure than baking for, or with, my friends. That, to me, sums up what the good life is really all about; sharing one's heart in a very practical and delicious way! And I have never met anyone who was not delighted to receive something baked 'from scratch', to use that lovely old-fashioned expression.

I've been blessed with many friends during my life, and every friendship is different, and inevitably comes with its own story. There is Althea, for example, whom I have known for more than 25 years, since we first lived in a shared house together in Johannesburg during the late 1980s. Inevitably, time has changed our lifestyles, and there are stretches when we don't see each other for several months, or even years at a time. But nothing changes the heart of the friendship, which remains as strong and honest as ever.

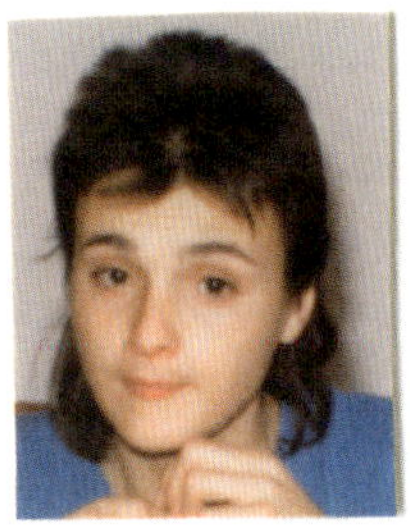

Friends are part of the glue that holds life and faith together. Powerful stuff.

JON KATZ

There are, sadly, a few special friends who are no longer with me, although their presence remains with me; just the form has changed. They are, hopefully, still with me in the kitchen when I bake, often using recipes that they shared with me many years ago. And then there are the new people we meet along the way, some of whom will also become friends, if we just open our hearts to them. Sometimes we all seem to be rushing around so much that contacts become both sporadic and superficial. It's nice, at times, to slow down and take time to talk to someone new, to learn something about his or her life. It could be the start of a beautiful friendship!

I've sometimes baked a cake, or cookies, for someone I hardly knew, someone who served me in a restaurant, or who works in a bookshop I go into (far more often than is good for my bank balance!). It's such a simple way to say 'thank you', or have a good day, or I see you as a person, not just an anonymous face.

OPPOSITE, ABOVE AND LEFT: Friends, old and new

Choc Chip Oatmeal Cookies

Quite simply, yummy! Just what one needs when the cookie monster strikes in the middle of the night. My mom originally found a version of this recipe in an American magazine, but she has since made some changes. I tend to chop up a bar of chocolate as I prefer that to the ready-made chips available. You can use dark, milk or white chocolate – whichever you prefer. Some chopped pecans or macadamias add tasty extra crunch. And this is a great recipe for introducing children to baking; with a little help they can turn out something really delicious.

250 ml (80 g) rolled oats
200 ml (110 g) cake flour
3 ml bicarbonate of soda
160 ml (130 g) light brown sugar
125 g butter, softened
1 egg
5 ml vanilla extract
175 g chopped chocolate (or choc chips)

Preheat the oven to 180 °C. Grease and line a large baking sheet with baking paper.

Mix the oats, flour and bicarbonate of soda together in a bowl. Cream the sugar and butter together well. Stir in the egg and vanilla. Add the oats mixture until just blended. Stir in the chocolate. Drop rounded tablespoons of dough onto the prepared baking sheet, ensuring that there is plenty of room for spreading.

Bake for 12–15 minutes, until the cookies are golden-brown. Leave to cool on a wire rack then store in an airtight tin or jar.

Makes ±15–20

What you see before you, my friend,
is the result of a lifetime of chocolate.

KATHERINE HEPBURN

Coconut Drops

Simply sweet, a traditional taste I remember from long ago. Also known as coconut macaroons, they were ubiquitous in old-fashioned bakeries, topped with a sticky red cherry. Children will also enjoy helping you to make them. (These days I prefer to drizzle the drops with a little melted dark chocolate after baking.)

1 egg, separated and 1 extra egg white
125 ml (105 g) castor sugar
5 ml vanilla essence
60 ml (35 g) cake flour
500 ml (160 g) desiccated coconut
glacé cherries, chopped (optional)
melted dark chocolate (optional)

Preheat the oven to 150 °C. Grease one large baking sheet very well.

Beat the egg yolk, sugar and vanilla together well. Stir in the flour and coconut. Beat the egg whites until stiff, then fold gently into the coconut mixture. Drop peaks of the mixture onto the prepared baking sheet and top each with a piece of cherry (if using).

Bake for 15 minutes, then reduce the oven temperature to 100 °C and bake for another 20–30 minutes, until golden-brown. Loosen the drops with a spatula and leave to cool on the baking sheet. Drizzle a little chocolate over the tops if you like. They will keep in an airtight container for 10 days.

Makes ±20

Be not afraid, but let your world be lit by miracles.

A COURSE IN MIRACLES

Sunshine Lemon Bars

Shortbread layers sandwich a tangy yet sweet lemon filling ... these are easy-to-make bar cookies that are delicious treats any time of the day, especially with a cup of tea!

125 g butter, softened
60 ml (50 g) castor sugar
375 ml (210 g) sifted cake flour
60 ml (20 g) fine desiccated coconut
3 ml salt

FILLING
385 g can condensed milk
1 egg
80 ml fresh lemon juice
finely grated zest of half a lemon
icing sugar for dusting

Preheat the oven to 180 °C. Grease a 23-cm square baking pan well.

Cream the butter and sugar together until fluffy and light, then stir in the flour, coconut and salt. Mix to form a fairly firm dough. Form about one-third of the dough into a ball, and refrigerate for 30 minutes.

Press the remaining dough evenly over the base of the prepared pan, and bake for 5–10 minutes, until just golden. Leave to cool in the pan briefly.

To make the filling, whisk together the condensed milk, egg, lemon juice and zest (the mixture will thicken a bit). Spread evenly over the cooled base. Coarsely grate the chilled portion of the dough over the filling. Bake for 25–35 minutes, until the topping is golden-brown. Leave to cool in the pan, then dust with icing sugar and cut into 5-cm squares.

Makes ±16

Saved by a Scone

It was a dark and stormy night ... And we were driving somewhere in the Scottish Highlands, although neither of us were quite sure where, given the heavy rain and the fact that I am not the best map reader in the world. It was September – a month for good weather, but not this September. Although this was supposed to be a camping holiday (my first and last!), quite clearly camping was not an option for that night.

Fortunately, we came upon a rather bleak house, standing alone at the side of a loch, like something out of a Robert Louis Stevenson novel. And there was a sign on the gate that proclaimed 'Bed and Breakfast'. The lady of the house was rather dour and unwelcoming, to put it mildly, but she did at least allow us in, to a room that was almost as chilly as her manner. When Terry asked, hesitantly, about a meal, she informed him that she did not provide food in the evenings, but would give us a few small scones, and a pot of tea, in the living room. Better than nothing, we supposed, and at least there was a fire in that room, unlike the bedroom.

Eilean Donan Castle, Loch Duich, Scottish Highlands

'The Loch Ness Monster', Loch Ness, southwest of Inverness

I have never, from that day to this, eaten scones like that – each one was the size of a baby's head, golden-brown, soft and flaky. With them was a bowl of gleaming bramble preserves, and another of creamy farm butter. We devoured those scones, washing them down with cups of strong tea, and felt totally reborn. I plucked up the courage to ask our hostess how she made her scones. 'Just flour, butter, salt and cream from the farm,' she said. I didn't dare ask for the recipe. But I was determined to recreate those scones, one day. And I think I did. Eventually.

Just a small, simple incident, really, but one that shows how everyday situations, even those that look distinctly unpromising, can hold some little gift or surprise or grace to remember.

You're off to the Great Plains, today is your day,
your mountain is waiting, so, get on your way.

DR SEUSS

Cherry Almond Scones

No rolling or cutting out is required for these as they are simply spooned onto a baking sheet. They're really more like rock cakes than scones; moist and crumbly, with the happy taste of cherries and almonds. (Do not use glacé cherries as they are not as nice as chopped maraschino or dried cherries.) Serve with lots of butter and a bowl of thick cream.

- 500 ml (280 g) cake flour
- 10 ml baking powder
- 3 ml salt
- 90 g cold butter, cubed
- 125 g chopped maraschino cherries, well drained, or dried cherries
- 60 ml slivered almonds
- 60 ml (50 g) castor sugar
- 1 egg
- 60 ml milk
- brown sugar for sprinkling

Preheat the oven to 200 °C. Grease a large baking sheet well.

Sift the flour, baking powder and salt together in a mixing bowl. Rub in the cold butter with your fingertips until the mixture resembles fine breadcrumbs. Mix in the cherries and 45 ml of the almonds. Stir in the sugar. Beat the egg and milk together then add to the cherry mixture, to form a fairly stiff dough. Use 2 spoons to place 8–10 mounds of the dough on the prepared baking sheet. Sprinkle with the remaining almonds and a little brown sugar. Bake for 15–20 minutes until golden-brown. Leave to cool briefly on a wire rack. These taste best when they are fresh.

Makes 8–10

You can either practise being right or practise being kind.

ANNE LAMOTT

Scottish Cream Scones

This is not the actual recipe for the cream scones we had in Scotland – see 'Saved by a scone' on page 114, but I have experimented since then, and I think these come pretty close. They're so simple, and taste wonderful just about any time of the day, served with lots of jam, honey and butter.

500 ml (280 g) cake flour	**65 g butter**
10 ml baking powder	**30 ml (25 g) castor sugar**
3 ml salt	**160 ml cream**

Preheat the oven to 200 °C. Grease a large baking sheet well.

Sift the flour, baking powder and salt into a large mixing bowl. Using your fingertips, rub in the butter until the mixture resembles fine breadcrumbs. Mix in the sugar. Make a well in the centre, and pour in the cream. Mix gently to make a soft, but not sticky, dough. If the mixture seems dry, add a little cold water; if it is sticky, sprinkle in a little extra flour. Turn the dough onto a floured board, and shape into a round, approximately 23 cm in diameter, and 1 cm high. Lift the round onto the prepared baking sheet, and use a palette knife to mark the dough lightly into 10–12wedges. Brush the scone round with a little milk or egg if you want a more golden crust, and bake for 10–15 minutes, until pale golden-brown and well risen. Leave to cool briefly, then cut the wedges as marked. Serve very fresh, and warm, if possible!

Makes 10-12

The greatest step towards a life of simplicity is to learn to let go ...

STEVE MARABOLI

Sharing the Sweetness

When I was very young, around three years old, my mother was seriously ill in hospital for quite a while. Obviously I don't remember much about that time, but one clear memory I do have, even decades later, is of a day I spent with my great-aunt Rosie, who lived in a small pink Victorian cottage in Sunnyside, near the river. We made scones for tea and I was allowed to help, first mixing the soft, buttery dough in a blue-and-white Cornishware bowl, then patting it out before my great-aunt cut out the scones and baked them.

That was probably my first baking memory and since then there have been so many, because I was (and am) lucky enough to have a mom who loved to cook and bake, and who also had the time and patience to share this with her daughter. The many, many hours we spent together in the kitchen remain a very special and treasured part of my childhood, not just for the practical skills I learned, but for the sense of continuity, and of being able to do something special for myself and others.

My mom, queen of the kitchen

Yours truly, around the time my baking 'career' started!

Nothing you do for children is ever wasted.

GARRISON KEILLOR

I certainly remember how proud I was when I turned out my first batch of cheese straws all by myself, for my mom's teatime guests, or made her famous cheesecake for a special party. And I think I must have been eleven when I first developed my lifelong love of cookbooks, reading them as if they were novels!

Cooking and baking are such hands-on activities, and healthy antidotes to the electronically driven lifestyles that so many of us (even children) tend to live these days. They're practical too, because anyone who can cook will always be able to take good care of themselves and others; in fact, they will probably have lots of friends!

So, if you have the chance to bake and cook with children – be they your own or someone else's – jump right in. You'll not only be giving them the gift of your time and attention, but lessons in the sweetness of being able to create something delicious from scratch, all by themselves. What a lovely memory to carry, tucked up in one of life's apron pockets.

The Best Apple Crumble

This delicious traditional pudding, which also goes by the name of apple crisp or cobbler, just tastes so warm and welcoming. My mother has been making it for me for years, from an old family recipe, and I can still taste the love in every bite! The coconut makes it extra special, but if you don't like coconut, just leave it out. Another really delicious addition is a handful of raisins or fresh blackberries, sprinkled over the apples before you add the topping.

Truth is like the sun ... you can shut it out for a while, but it ain't going anywhere.

ELVIS PRESLEY

125 ml (140 g) cake flour	250 ml (80 g) desiccated coconut
3 ml baking powder	125 g butter, cubed
200 ml (170 g) castor sugar	185 g can pie apples

Preheat the oven to 180 °C. Grease a medium baking dish well.

Combine the flour, baking powder, sugar and coconut in a bowl. Rub in the butter until the mixture resembles coarse breadcrumbs. Sprinkle half of this dough into the bottom of the prepared baking dish. Cover with the apples. Top with the remaining dough. Bake for 30 minutes, until the topping is brown and crisp. Serve with lots of vanilla custard or whipped cream.

Serves 4–6

Mocha Crumble Cake

Coffee and chocolate – a divine taste combination, and even better in this simple yet delicious cake, that is a breeze to make. I love this type of cake, moist and a little bit like pudding! Serve plain for breakfast or brunch, or topped with whipped cream at tea time.

- 125 g butter, softened
- 200 ml (170 g) castor sugar
- 5 ml vanilla extract
- 2 eggs
- 250 ml (140 g) cake flour
- 5 ml baking powder
- 5 ml bicarbonate of soda
- 3 ml salt
- 250 ml sour cream
- 15 ml strong black coffee

CRUMBLE TOPPING

- 125 ml (70 g) cake flour, sifted
- 125 ml (100 g) brown sugar
- 3 ml salt
- 125 g butter, cubed
- 125 ml (100 g) chocolate chips

First make the crumble topping. Combine the flour, brown sugar and salt in a bowl. Rub in the butter with your fingertips until the mixture resembles breadcrumbs. Stir in the chocolate chips, then set aside.

Preheat the oven to 180 °C. Grease a 23-cm square cake pan.

For the cake, cream the butter and castor sugar together until pale and creamy. Add the vanilla and eggs, one at a time. In another bowl, sift the flour, baking powder, bicarbonate of soda and salt together. Add to the butter mixture in three batches, alternating with the sour cream. Lastly beat in the coffee. Spoon into the prepared pan and sprinkle evenly with the crumble topping. Bake for 35–40 minutes until a tester comes out clean, then leave to cool on a wire rack.

Serves 6–8

Those who don't believe in magic will never find it.

ROALD DAHL

Little Tea Cakes

Not really cakes at all, these are more like soft, buttery cookies. This is a very old recipe with the kind of simple elegance I love. The little tea cakes also make a wonderful gift; pile them in a colourful box lined with tissue paper, and tie up with lots of curly ribbon. I have suggested raspberry jam as the filling because it is my personal favourite, but other options include strawberry, apricot or cherry jam, or lemon curd, or even a teaspoon of caramel condensed milk.

185 g butter, softened
60 ml (35 g) icing sugar
3 ml vanilla extract
30 ml cornflour
250 ml (140 g) cake flour
5 ml baking powder
jam or preserves
extra icing sugar for dusting

Preheat the oven to 180 °C. Line 24 small (5-cm) muffin pan cups with pretty paper cups.

Cream the butter, icing sugar and vanilla together. Add the cornflour, cake flour and baking powder, and mix to form a soft dough. Roll the dough into approximately 4-cm balls, and place one in each paper cup. Use the handle of a wooden spoon to make an indentation in the centre of each ball. Bake for 15–20 minutes, until very pale gold in colour. Leave to cool for 20 minutes, then drop a teaspoon of jam (or preserve) into the hole of each tea cake. Dust the cakes generously with icing sugar. Leave to cool completely before serving.

Makes ±24

Be happy. It's one way of being wise.

COLETTE

Dorset Apple Cake

Apples are such simple, happy and delicious fruit, it's hard not to like anything that's made with them. In England, apple cake is a popular use for them, served either for tea or as a pudding, warm with cream. I confess to having eaten my fair share of apple cake there – purely in the interests of research, of course – and I think this recipe is a good representative of the best in apple cake! Use lovely fresh, ripe, eating apples.

500 ml (280 g) cake flour
5 ml baking powder
5 ml bicarbonate of soda
10 ml ground cinnamon
3 ml salt
125 ml (75 g) chopped walnuts
125 ml (75 g) seedless raisins
125 g butter, softened
250 ml (100 g) light brown sugar
10 ml vanilla extract
3 extra large eggs
2 large apples, peeled, cored and chopped into small chunks

Preheat the oven to 180 °C. Grease a deep 25-cm cake pan and line the base with baking paper.

Sift the flour, baking powder, bicarbonate of soda, cinnamon and salt together. In another bowl, mix the nuts and raisins (sprinkle them with a little flour if the raisins are sticky). In a large mixing bowl, beat the butter, sugar and vanilla together until the mixture is light and creamy. Beat in the eggs, one at a time. Add the flour mixture alternately with the apples, until the batter is well-blended. Lastly, stir in the nuts and raisins. Use a spatula to spread the batter in the prepared pan, then bake for 40–45 minutes, until a tester comes out clean. Leave to cool in the pan for a while, then turn out onto a wire rack. The cake can be served warm with custard, as a pudding, or left to cool completely and served with thick cream at tea time. (It keeps well for a couple of days, if stored in an airtight container at room temperature.)

Serves 10–12

When you do things from your soul,
you feel a river moving in you, a joy ...

RUMI

Cottage Pudding with Lemon Sauce

The simple taste of a childhood pudding, sweet and comforting, this is basically a cake – quick and easy to prepare, served with a tangy lemon sauce. Ideal winter food! You can use orange for the sauce if you prefer and the brandy can also be replaced with fruit juice.

450 ml (250 g) cake flour
10 ml baking powder
3 ml salt
60 g butter, softened
200 ml (170 g) castor sugar
1 egg
5 ml vanilla extract
200 ml milk or buttermilk

LEMON SAUCE
250 ml (210 g) castor sugar
30 ml cornflour
375 ml water
30 ml brandy
juice and rind of 1 small lemon
60 g butter

Preheat the oven to 180 °C. Grease a 23-cm baking dish well.

Sift the flour, baking powder and salt together in a bowl. Cream the butter and 200 ml sugar together, then mix in the egg and vanilla. Add the flour mixture and milk or buttermilk, beating well to form a smooth batter. Pour into the prepared dish and bake for 25–30 minutes until well risen and golden. Serve warm, cut into squares, with lots of lemon sauce!

To make the lemon sauce, mix the 250 ml sugar and cornflour in a saucepan. Stir in the water and bring to the boil, stirring constantly. Stir in the brandy, lemon juice and rind, and butter. When the sauce is smooth and thick, remove from heat and serve.

Serves 4–6

There are big ships and small ships ... but the best ship of all is friendship.

ANON

Brandy Raisin Bread Pudding

This is an old favourite that has been given a little bit of a twist with the brandied raisins. My mother used to make it as one of the regular desserts for the retreat house in England where she worked, and the plates were always licked clean – even by the so-called tee-totalers, who probably wondered what made the pudding taste so good! You can use perfectly ordinary white sliced bread for this, but I prefer to use slices from a large French loaf instead.

125 ml (75 g) raisins
60 ml brandy
butter, for spreading
10 thin slices of bread (see above)
250 ml milk
250 ml fresh cream
5 ml vanilla extract
3 ml salt
3 eggs, beaten
125 ml (105 g) castor sugar

Some people feel the rain. Others just get wet.

BOB MARLEY

The day before you plan to make the bread pudding, cover the raisins with the brandy in a small bowl and soak overnight.

The next day, preheat the oven to 170 °C; and thoroughly grease an oval or rectangular baking dish with a capacity of about 1.1 litres. Butter the slices of bread and then cut in half (cut off or retain the crusts, as you prefer). Warm the milk and cream together with the vanilla and salt, until hot but not boiling. Remove from the heat. Beat the eggs and sugar together in a large bowl, then whisk in the warm milk mixture.

Arrange half the slices of bread on the bottom of the prepared dish, and sprinkle with half the soaked raisins (include any leftover brandy liquid). Top with the remaining bread slices and raisins. Pour the egg custard mixture carefully over the bread, ensuring all the bread is moistened and covered. Stand the baking dish in a large roasting dish that has been half-filled with water; and bake for 35–40 minutes, until the pudding is firm and golden. Serve warm, with more cream or thick vanilla custard.

Serves 4–6

A little of what you fancy ...

Let's be clear, I am not, and never have been, very interested in so-called 'healthy eating'; it wasn't really an issue when I was young, because we ate a balanced diet of good, fresh food, and sweet things were a treat for special occasions, not something to be munched on every day. Strangely, I also don't remember any of my childhood friends being overweight, something that sadly is not always true of children today.

A few people suggested to me that a baking book filled with recipes for things containing lots of butter, sugar, chocolate and eggs was perhaps a bad idea. I really don't agree with them. Obviously, if you are going to eat an entire chocolate cake at one sitting, something will have to give – probably the waistband on your jeans! But – and here I quote from my favourite Australian cookbook author, Belinda Jeffery – 'a slice of cake never made anyone fat, and it certainly makes them happy.' My philosophy exactly.

I believe in the principle of eating what you want, just eating less of it. One scone or slice of toast instead of two, one (smaller) spoon of pudding, and so on. The best thing is, you'll never feel deprived as you will still be able to eat everything you enjoy. Maybe this is not sound dietary advice, but it certainly works for me. (Admittedly, I am lucky because although I love baking things, I don't have much of a sweet tooth, so I tend not to eat too much of the finished product.)

Once again, the key is balance – and awareness. Good lessons for life in general.

I am not overweight. I am under tall.

MISS PIGGY

Jiffy Cheese Biscuits

Actually what we know as scones, but as the original recipe for these (which I have since tweaked somewhat) came from an American magazine I thought I would keep the first name. Not really traditional scones either, but they're certainly a winner as far as taste and instant gratification go! They're delicious served with lots of butter, either for breakfast or tea, or as part of a cosy kitchen supper alongside a steaming pot of soup or stew. To vary the flavour, add a tablespoon of finely snipped herbs (chives or parsley are nice), and half a teaspoon of finely minced garlic or chilli.

500 ml (280 g) cake flour
15 ml baking powder
5 ml salt
200 ml (75 g) grated Cheddar cheese
1 egg
125 ml water
125 ml buttermilk
65 g butter, melted and cooled
ground paprika (optional)

Preheat the oven to 220 °C and grease a large baking sheet.

Sift the flour, baking powder and salt together in a large bowl. Stir in the cheese. In another bowl, whisk together the egg, water, buttermilk and melted butter. Make a well in the centre of the dry ingredients, and pour in the liquid. Using a fork, mix quickly to form a soft dough. (It should be manageable, but not sticky!)

Using 2 spoons, drop mounds of dough onto the prepared baking sheet, and dust the tops lightly with the paprika, if using. Bake for 10–15 minutes, until golden-brown. Leave to cool on a wire rack. They are best served warm, on the day they are made, which is not exactly a hardship!

Makes 10–12

Write it on your heart … that every day is the best day of the year!

RW EMERSON

Althea's Pizza Muffins

Althea – one of my dearest friends – loves pizza in any and all of its guises, but she isn't all that keen on baking, so I thought these muffins would be quite a hit with her. This is really a spontaneous kind of recipe, in that you can add different ingredients, according to taste. Bacon, or slivers of ham, for example, or herbs. Basil would actually be more authentic, but I don't care for it, which is why I tend to use oregano. Just one word of warning – I once added some chopped anchovies, in a misguided moment, and I can assure you that fishy muffins really aren't that nice!

750 ml (420 g) cake flour
15 ml baking powder
5 ml salt
15 ml grated Parmesan cheese
2 eggs
125 ml sunflower oil
250 ml milk
125 ml (150 g) sun-dried tomatoes (drained if in oil), chopped small
5 ml crushed garlic
65 g stoned black olives, chopped small
125 ml (60 g) mozzarella cheese, cut into small cubes
30 ml chopped fresh oregano

Preheat the oven to 200 °C. Grease a 12-cup regular muffin pan well.

Mix the flour, baking powder, salt and Parmesan in a large bowl, then set aside. In another bowl, beat the eggs, oil and milk. Stir the egg mixture into the flour until just combined (don't over-beat; mixture should still be a bit lumpy). Stir in the tomatoes, garlic, olives, mozzarella and oregano. Spoon the mixture into the muffin pan cups, filling each about two-thirds. Bake for 20 minutes, until firm and golden-brown. They are best served warm with lots of butter, or as a side dish with a hearty soup or a fresh salad.

Makes 12

Why fit in, when you were born to stand out?

DR SEUSS

Spicy Biltong Muffins

There is a tendency these days for muffins to be absolutely gargantuan, which is a pity since smaller muffins are nicer, in my opinion (quite apart from being a little healthier). I've been making variations of biltong muffins for years, but my recipe really kicked up a notch when I read a recipe for biltong muffins published in a You *cookbook, about ten years ago, from Niel Stemmet, who had a restaurant called Le Must in the heart of the Kalahari. His biltong was marinated in sherry, before being added to the muffin batter, and it is just wonderful. So, thank you to him for this great idea! (Instead of the Cheddar, you can also use mild blue cheese.) These muffins are delicious any time of the day, and especially so when served with lots of unsalted butter and cream cheese.*

There's a crack in everyone. That's how the light gets in.

LEONARD COHEN

- 250 ml thinly sliced, lean biltong
- 30 ml dry sherry
- 500 ml (280 g) cake flour
- 10 ml baking powder
- 5 ml salt
- 3 ml peri-peri spice
- 250 ml buttermilk
- 2 eggs
- 80 ml oil
- 15 ml minced onion
- 5 ml minced chilli (optional)
- 125 ml (50 g) grated Cheddar cheese

Preheat the oven to 190 °C. Grease a 12-cup regular muffin pan very well.

About an hour before you plan to make the muffins, finely chop the biltong, then marinate it in the sherry.

Mix together the flour, baking powder, salt and peri-peri in a large bowl. In another bowl, beat together the buttermilk, eggs, oil, onion and chilli (if using). Make a well in the centre of the dry ingredients and pour in the buttermilk mixture. Mix quickly with a wooden spoon, then stir in the biltong and sherry mixture, as well as the cheese. Mix again briefly, just enough to ensure the batter is blended. Divide the batter among the cups of the prepared muffin pan and bake for 15–20 minutes, until the muffins are golden-brown and firm. Leave to cool briefly in the pan, then turn out onto a wire rack to finish cooling.

Serve warm or cold. The muffins will keep in an airtight container for a couple of days.

Makes 12 regular muffins

Cranks Cheese Tart

Cranks was a chain of health food restaurants in London when I lived there. They were enormously popular and usually packed out for lunch or supper. Quite honestly, I am not big on healthy eating, but my boyfriend was, and so we often stopped in there for a quick meal. This cheese tart is probably one of the fastest recipes in the book; it appeared in one of the cookbooks published by the restaurant chain. I have changed it a little, and I tend to add ingredients such as bacon pieces or well-drained asparagus. Be sure to use fresh breadcrumbs.

I may not have gone where I intended to go,
but I think I have ended up where I needed to be.

DOUGLAS ADAMS

375 ml (90 g) fresh breadcrumbs (white or wholewheat)
375 ml milk
250 ml (100 g) grated strong Cheddar cheese
3 ml salt
half a small onion, grated
3 ml black pepper
2 large eggs
15 ml chopped fresh parsley

Preheat the oven to 200 °C. Grease a medium round or rectangular baking dish well.

Combine all the ingredients in a large bowl (or a food processor) and beat together very well. Pour into the prepared baking dish, and bake for about 20 minutes, until golden-brown and puffed up. Serve hot.

Serves 4–6

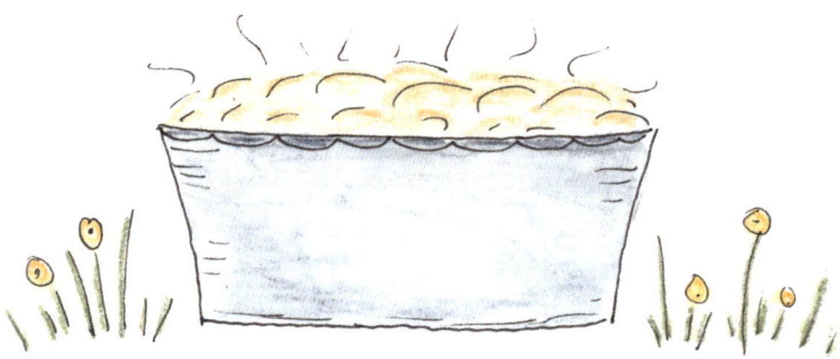

Wholewheat Irish Soda Bread

I have never been to Ireland, although from what I have heard of it, I think it would suit me just fine, being a somewhat quirky and different place. This recipe came from a nun at the convent school I attended; she was probably already in her eighties then, but had such humour and charm, even when dealing with teenage schoolgirls. She often told us about her childhood growing up on a farm in Kerry, and the simple life they led; this type of bread was apparently a staple at most meals. I like it because it's quick and easy – no yeast – and can be eaten with just about anything or any meal, or just spread thickly with butter and jam.

Ever notice how 'what the hell' is always the right answer?

MARILYN MONROE

750 ml (420 g) white cake flour
250 ml (140 g) wholewheat flour
10 ml baking powder
5 ml salt
60 g unsalted butter
1 egg
375 ml buttermilk
125 ml (75 g) seedless raisins (optional)

Preheat the oven to 180 °C. Grease a medium baking sheet.

Sift the flours, baking powder and salt together in a large bowl. Using your fingertips, rub in the butter until the mixture resembles large breadcrumbs. Beat together the egg and buttermilk, and pour this into the flour mixture. Add the raisins, if using. Mix well to form a firm, but not stiff dough. Form into a round measuring ±20 cm in diameter, and lift onto the prepared baking sheet. Using a sharp knife cut a 1-cm deep cross into the top of the loaf. Bake for 50–60 minutes, until a tester inserted in the centre of the loaf comes out clean. Turn out onto a wire rack, right side up, to cool. This bread is really best on the day it is made, although you can keep it, wrapped, for another day or two.

Serves 8

Little Herb Pikelets

'Pikelets' is just an old term for little pancakes; actually, these small yeast pancakes are more akin to Russian blini (minus the buckwheat flour). They look really charming arranged on a plate, topped with cream cheese and a rose of smoked salmon or trout. A friend of mine tops hers with thin slices of smoked ham and mustard; for brunch try a dollop of creamy scrambled eggs and chopped chives. Use any herbs such as parsley, thyme, chives, oregano or dill. Or the savoury toppings can be omitted, thus making the pikelets suitable for sweet toppings such as soft fruits or honey.

10 g fresh yeast (or 5 ml dried)
5 ml granulated white sugar
250 ml milk, warmed
15 ml (±10 g) cake flour
250 ml (140 g) cake flour
3 ml salt
1 egg
30 ml melted butter
30 ml chopped fresh herbs

Success is liking yourself, liking what you do, and liking how you do it.

MAYA ANGELOU

Cream together the fresh yeast and sugar (or combine the sugar with the dried yeast), then add the warm milk to the yeast mixture and stir well. Sprinkle over the 15 ml flour, cover and leave to stand for 20 minutes, until the mixture is bubbly. In another mixing bowl, sift the 250 ml flour and salt together. Stir in the yeast batter, egg and butter, then beat to form a smooth batter. Lastly fold in the chopped herbs. Cover the bowl and leave to stand in a warm place for about 45 minutes, or until the batter has almost doubled in bulk. Beat again before cooking the pancakes.

Heat a heavy-bottomed frying pan with a knob of butter, until moderately hot. Drop 3 separate tablespoonfuls of the batter into the pan (be careful as they do spread). Cook for 2 minutes, or until bubbles appear on top of the pancakes. Turn carefully with a spatula and cook for about 3 minutes on the other side, until the pancakes are golden-brown. Cook in batches, keeping the completed pancakes covered and warm. Serve warm or cold, but preferably as fresh as possible.

Makes ±16

Spicy Pumpkin Puffs

To be quite honest, I have never been a huge fan of vegetables, but pumpkins are an exception. We used to have a roast lunch on Sundays, usually lamb, but sometimes chicken or beef; alongside the meat were always slices of roast pumpkin, soft and golden, and a little brown and sticky on the edges, where they had absorbed some of the meat juice. In winter, too, there was the comfort of bowls of my mom's creamy pumpkin soup. But pumpkin fritters were by far my favourite – I loved making them, and eating them even more! However, some time back, I decided to experiment with a different way of preparing pumpkin – like fritters, but baked, not fried. Quick, easy and delicious with dinner, or at a braai, or just eaten as a finger-food snack.

250 ml (140 g) cake flour
10 ml baking powder
5 ml salt
5 ml ground cinnamon
30 ml light brown sugar
1 egg
60 ml buttermilk
250 ml smooth mashed pumpkin

My favourite word is 'pumpkin'. You are a pumpkin or you are not. I am.

HARRISON SALISBURY

Preheat the oven to 180 °C. Grease a 12-cup shallow muffin pan very well.

Sift together the flour, baking powder, salt, cinnamon and sugar. In another bowl, beat the egg and buttermilk together lightly, then stir into the pumpkin. Stir the dry ingredients into the pumpkin mixture, and mix to a batter. Divide the batter equally into the muffin cups – you may find you can make more than 12, depending on the size. (It's nice to sprinkle a little extra brown sugar and cinnamon over each.) Bake for 15–20 minutes, or until the puffs have set and are golden-brown at the edges. Leave to cool in the pan for a short while before transferring them to a rack. These are best served warm, and fresh.

Makes 12 (or more)

Onion and Herb Quick Bread

Simply delicious, this is one of those stand-by recipes that never seem to go out of fashion. The bread is wonderful with soup, or a braai, or any rib-sticking winter meal! I am not generally a big fan of packet soups, but this is one exception; instead of the cream of onion soup you can use the brown onion flavour, if you prefer. The herbs are also a matter of personal preference; I like chives (which pick up nicely on the onion flavour), parsley, thyme or oregano. Try to use fresh herbs – they make a big difference to the finished bread.

1 litre (560 g) cake flour
20 ml baking powder
5 ml salt
1 packet cream of onion soup powder
1 egg
500 ml buttermilk
30 ml finely chopped fresh herbs (your choice)

Wheresoever you go, go with all your heart.

KONGZI

Preheat the oven to 190 °C. Grease 1 large or 2 medium loaf pans well.

Mix the flour, baking powder, salt and soup powder in a large bowl. Beat the egg and buttermilk together, then add to the flour mixture. Mix well, to form a sticky dough. Stir in the chopped herbs. Spoon the batter into the prepared pan(s). Turn the oven down to 180 °C and bake for approximately 1 hour (large loaf) or 45 minutes (medium loaves), until well risen and golden, and a tester comes out clean. Leave to cool briefly in the pans, then turn out onto a wire rack. The bread tastes best served on the day it is baked.

Makes 1 large, or 2 medium loaves

Fastest Pizza in Town

Not one for the purists, probably, but this easy pizza dough tastes good and everyone seems to like it. When I worked with children some years back, and we cooked together, this was always a favourite recipe with them. Part of the fun, of course, is that everyone can choose their own toppings, and create their own unique pizza. This recipe also originates from my mother, who found it in the old Betty Crocker cookbook we had at home. For those of you who don't know, Betty Crocker was a creation of an American food company, who dreamed her up as the perfect cook and homemaker. I was quite upset when I finally realised that she had never existed! (I have changed the recipe a little, and I now use olive oil, which I think gives a slightly more authentic flavour to the pizza crust.)

The only real stumbling block is fear of failing.
In cooking you've got to have a what-the-hell attitude.

JULIA CHILD

500 ml (280 g) cake flour
10 ml baking powder
5 ml salt
160 ml milk
60 ml olive oil
125 ml tomato purée
5 ml crushed garlic
5 ml ground black pepper
your choice of toppings (sliced mozzarella, crumbled feta, anchovies, olives, ham, mushrooms, salami, asparagus, spinach, prawns, avocado, bacon, pineapple)

Preheat the oven to 220 °C. Grease a large pizza pan or baking sheet lightly.

Mix together the flour, baking powder and salt in a large bowl. Beat the milk and oil together, then pour into the flour mixture. Beat well, before turning out onto a floured surface. Knead until you have a soft yet manageable, but not sticky, dough. Press thinly and evenly into the prepared pizza pan or baking sheet.

Combine the tomato purée, garlic and pepper, and spread a thin layer of this over the dough. Then, add any toppings you like. Finish with a little extra garlic, and freshly ground pepper. Bake for 20–25 minutes, until the topping is bubbling hot, and the crust looks golden.

Serves 2–3

Food is our common ground,
a universal experience.

JAMES BEARD

When I was about eleven, my father gave my mother a gift of a subscription to a series published by Time Life Books, called *Foods of the World.* I think there were about 20 books in the series, and every two months or so another one would arrive – a large, hardcover book filled with photos, stories and recipes for the food of a particular country. These books were my absolute favourites – I would devour them, fascinated by the foods and the cultures. (In fact, I still have a few of them on my bookshelf!)

My poor mother also had to put up with me wanting to try out some of the recipes, but she was remarkably patient about it; some experiments were successful, others less so! But these books contributed to my lifelong interest in the food other people cook and bake, an interest that has grown and developed over time, partly because I have been lucky enough to travel to a number of different countries, and even spend time living in some of them. At home, so many of my friends come from different backgrounds and cultures, and all of them have something delicious to share as part of their heritage.

I find that food, and recipes, are usually the shortest distance between two people. Even if they don't know each other, sharing this simplest and most common bond of all, dissolves the sense that anyone is really a stranger. I've shared, and been given, recipes for puddings and cakes and breads in all sorts of settings, and by all sorts of people, sometimes even the most unlikely ones! (As, for example, the rather large gentleman with a Harley-Davidson I met at a Scottish tea shop, who insisted that his pancakes were the best in the world.)

Starting in our own backyards, there is always something new to taste, and delicious to discover, as we share in the gifts from other tables.

LeMae's Southern Pound Cake

LeMae was an American girl from the deep South (Arkansas), who I met in Pretoria in the early 1990s when I tutored her young son. I learnt much about the traditions and tastes of 'down home' southern cooking from her, and also discovered that Southerners certainly have a sweet tooth. She told me that this type of pound cake may even be served for breakfast, sliced and toasted! The really Southern part about it is probably the shot of whiskey (or bourbon), which adds a taste dimension to the cake, but you can use something else such as brandy or sherry if you prefer, or replace the alcohol with milk.

450 ml (250 g) cake flour
3 ml salt
5 ml baking powder
125 g butter, softened
250 ml (210 g) castor sugar
2 eggs
125 ml sour cream
5 ml vanilla extract
60 ml bourbon whiskey

Good food blesses all, the one who cooks it, and the one who eats it.

CAMILLE GLENN, COOKBOOK AUTHOR AND
DOYENNE OF TRADITIONAL SOUTHERN COOKING

Preheat the oven to 180 °C. Grease a large loaf pan very well.

In a medium bowl, sift together the flour, salt and baking powder. In a large bowl, cream the butter and sugar together until light and fluffy. Beat in the eggs, one at a time, until well blended. Stir in the sour cream, vanilla and whiskey, alternating with the dry ingredients, to form a thick and smooth batter. Pour the mixture into the prepared loaf pan. Bake for 45 minutes, or until the cake is risen and golden-brown, and a tester comes out clean. Leave to cool for 5 minutes, before turning out onto a wire rack.

Now for the fun part! Of course, you can simply slice the cake and eat it plain, but it can also be served alongside all sorts of delicious things such as ice cream, whipped cream and fresh, soft fruits (think strawberries or raspberries). Try drizzling it with some warm chocolate or caramel sauce. And then there's always breakfast ...

Makes 1 large loaf

Swedish Midsummer Cake

This probably isn't the correct name in Sweden, but I once knew a Swedish girl called Benedicte, who told me this was the cake her mom always made for her on her birthday, which happened to be in the middle of summer there. Actually, she made my mouth water with all her descriptions of delicious Scandinavian baking! And yet she was as thin and elegant as any model, despite the fact that she ate us all under the table. She also told me they sometimes used redcurrants instead of strawberries, but I think strawberries are nicest. It's just such a pretty, light and colourful cake, from a land where the sun almost never sets in summer.

- 3 eggs
- 160 ml (140 g) castor sugar
- 5 ml vanilla extract
- 250 ml (140 g) cake flour
- 8 ml baking powder

- 375 ml cream
- 30 ml castor sugar
- 250 g strawberries, hulled and sliced
- icing sugar for dusting

Be yourself. Everyone else is already taken.

OSCAR WILDE

Preheat the oven to 180 °C. Grease a fairly deep 25-cm cake pan well.

Using an electric mixer if possible, beat the eggs, 160 ml castor sugar and vanilla together for at least 8 minutes, until the mixture is thick and pale. Sift the flour and baking powder together then gently fold into the egg mixture. Pour the batter into the prepared cake pan, and bake for 25 minutes, until the sponge is well risen and golden-brown. Leave to cool briefly then turn out of the pan onto a wire rack until completely cold.

Shortly before you serve the cake, whip the cream until it forms soft peaks. Gently fold in the 30 ml of castor sugar. Using a sharp knife, carefully cut the cake into 3 equal layers, and place the bottom layer on a cake plate. Spread half the whipped cream onto this layer, then sprinkle with a third of the strawberries. Top with the next layer, and repeat the process. Cover with the third sponge, dust with icing sugar and decorate with the remaining strawberries. Serve as soon as possible.

Serves 10–12

Raspberry Pecan Coffee Cake

Another delicious – and fairly antique! – American recipe; they love their coffee cakes, and so do I, because they are not only quick and simple to prepare, but taste good any time of the day, from breakfast through to brunch, tea and even as dessert (with lots of cream, of course). The original recipe used fresh raspberries, but I find good quality raspberry preserve or jam works just as well, and is a little easier too. You can substitute strawberries, if you prefer. Sour cream, common in American baking, lends a subtle tang and fine texture to this cake.

500 ml (280 g) cake flour
10 ml baking powder
3 ml salt
125 g butter, softened
250 ml (210 g) castor sugar
2 eggs
5 ml vanilla extract
250 ml sour cream
250 ml raspberry preserve

PECAN STREUSEL
125 ml (75 g) finely chopped pecan nuts
60 ml (50 g) brown sugar
30 ml cake flour
5 ml ground cinnamon

Preheat the oven to 180 °C. Grease a fairly deep, 23-cm round cake pan well.

To make the streusel, mix the pecans with the brown sugar, flour, and cinnamon, then set aside.

For the cake, sift together the flour, baking powder and salt in a bowl. In another bowl, cream together the butter and sugar until light and fluffy, then stir in the eggs and vanilla. Add the dry ingredients in 3 or 4 batches, alternating with the sour cream, until the batter is well mixed. Place half the batter in the prepared cake pan, then carefully spread the raspberry preserve evenly over the top. Cover with the remaining batter, and level the top of the mixture. Sprinkle with the pecan streusel.

Bake for 35–40 minutes, until the cake is risen and golden-brown. Leave to cool in the pan for a few minutes, then turn out onto a wire rack. The cake will last, wrapped or stored in an airtight container, for several days.

Serves 6

People say nothing is impossible, but I do nothing every day.

WINNIE THE POOH (AA MILNE)

Cassata alla Siciliana

My father's family originally came from Italy, and my mother, although not Italian herself, learnt to cook many Italian specialities when they were married. (My dad's favourite has always been spaghetti served very simply with olive oil and garlic.) We also used to go to a little restaurant called Caffé Italia, which was always filled with a wonderful garlic aroma, and lit by candles stuck in old Chianti bottles. This was the cake they often produced for special occasions such as birthdays. When I was in my teens I discovered a recipe for it in an old cookbook, and started making it myself. It's a delicious alternative to the more usual celebration cakes, and is not too difficult, as you can even use a bought loaf cake (although it's nicer if you make it yourself). The chocolate icing is wonderfully rich and decadent. This cake should be served in small slices.

1 Madeira/loaf cake (10 x 28 cm)
250 ml (250 g) ricotta cheese
60 ml (50 g) castor sugar
125 ml thick cream
30 ml grappa (or brandy)
30 ml orange juice
65 g glacé fruits, chopped
65 g dark chocolate, chopped

CHOCOLATE ICING
250 g dark chocolate, chopped
125 ml strong black coffee
125 g chilled butter, cubed
60 ml (35 g) icing sugar

Rome's Trevi Fountain

The Grand Canal, Venice

There is only one journey. Going inside yourself.

RAINER MARIA RILKE

Trim the loaf cake so that the top is flat, not rounded. Cut it horizontally into three equal layers. Place the ricotta in a mixing bowl, and beat with a wooden spoon until smooth. Beating constantly, add the castor sugar, cream, brandy and orange juice. Fold in the chopped fruits and chocolate. Use this mixture to fill the 2 layers of the cake (not the top, which must be left plain). Don't worry if it seems a bit soft; wrap the cake in plastic wrap and refrigerate for 2 hours, after which time the filling will have firmed up.

For the icing, place the chocolate and coffee in a small glass bowl. Place over a saucepan of simmering water, and stir until the chocolate has melted completely. Remove from the heat, then gradually beat in the butter in small pieces, until the mixture is smooth. Stir in the icing sugar and beat again. Chill until the chocolate mixture is spreadable.
Using a spatula, cover the top and sides of the chilled cake with the icing. Cover loosely with a piece of aluminium foil, and chill again for at least 4–6 hours before serving.

Serves 8–10

Smiddy Loaf

My maternal grandmother's family originally came from Scotland, so perhaps that is why I love that country, and always have – ever since I went there as a little girl. It's wildly beautiful, full of drama and history, but the weather there can be, quite frankly, awful. Perhaps that is why the Scots also have such a wonderful baking tradition; after all, there's nothing nicer than spending a grey, miserable day baking in a cosy kitchen. The original recipe for this fruit loaf comes from a lovely little book, Scottish Recipe Book, *one in the 'Teapot Trail Series', and is named for the Old Smiddy Tea Room, Laide, in the Scottish Highlands.*

- 125 g butter
- 200 ml (160 g) dark brown sugar
- 375 g mixed dried fruit
- 250 ml water
- 5 ml bicarbonate of soda
- 5 ml cinnamon
- 5 ml mixed spice
- 500 ml (280 g) cake flour
- 10 ml baking powder
- 2 eggs, beaten

Preheat the oven to 180 °C. Grease a medium loaf pan well and line the base with baking paper.

Place the butter, sugar, dried fruit and water in a heavy-bottomed saucepan and bring to the boil. Simmer for a few minutes, then stir in the bicarbonate of soda and spices. Remove from the heat and leave the mixture to cool completely.

Sift together the flour and baking powder. Stir the eggs into the dried fruit mixture, followed by the flour and baking powder. Pour into the prepared pan and bake for 60–90 minutes, until risen and a tester comes out clean. (If the top starts to brown too much, cover loosely with aluminium foil.) Leave to cool completely before removing from the pan. It's best to wrap the loaf in foil for a day or two before serving. Serve thickly sliced and buttered.

Serves 6–8

Scotland has just two seasons: June and winter.

BILLY CONNOLLY

Petits Mokatines de Paris

I was fortunate enough to visit Paris once, a long time ago, when I was still quite young, but that brief visit has stayed with me, and I hope to return one day. Of course, there are so many things to remember about that timeless city, but typically, food figures prominently in my memories. The meals certainly, and the vibrant food markets, but I particularly remember the bakeries, and salons du thé, with their casual elegance and delicious patisserie. *This recipe is based on the traditional Genoese sponge, which is used to make charming little cakes, topped with rich butter-cream. (By the way, butter-cream is not particularly cheap or quick to make, but when you taste it you will definitely agree that it is worth it!)*

GENOESE SPONGE

250 ml (210 g) castor sugar
4 eggs
5 ml vanilla extract
250 ml (140 g) cake flour
3 ml baking powder
125 g butter, melted and cooled

MOCHA BUTTER-CREAM

250 ml (210 g) castor sugar
80 ml water
3 egg yolks
125 g butter, softened
30 ml instant coffee granules dissolved in 15 ml hot water, then cooled

DECORATION

chopped almonds or grated chocolate

Paris is always a good idea.

AUDREY HEPBURN

Preheat the oven to 180 °C. Grease a 23-cm square cake pan well.

For the sponge, in a large bowl beat the castor sugar and eggs together very well (preferably with an electric mixer) until the mixture is very thick and pale. Stir in the vanilla. In another bowl, sift the flour and baking powder together, then gradually add to the egg mixture, folding in very gently with a wooden spoon. Lastly, fold in the melted butter. Pour the batter into the prepared pan, then bake for 30 minutes, or until the cake is golden and a tester comes out clean. Turn out onto a wire rack to cool completely.

To make the butter-cream, combine the sugar and water in a small saucepan, and boil rapidly until the liquid has reduced by half, and a syrup has formed. In another bowl, beat the egg yolks until creamy and pale, then very gradually beat in the warm syrup, to form a fairly thick mixture. Beat the butter into the mixture, in small amounts. Lastly, stir in the coffee.

Cut 16.5-cm circles from the cooled cake, and place each mini cake in a paper case. Ice with the mocha butter-cream, piping it on if you want a more decorative look. Decorate with chopped almonds or grated chocolate. Eat within a day or two; butter-cream does not last well.

Makes 16

A Little Country Comfort

When I lived in England for a number of years, some of that time was spent in a small market town not far from Oxford, on the doorstep of the Cotswolds, one of the most beautiful and picturesque parts of the country. Almost every weekend we would drive to a different area, and spend our time taking in the charming scenery, the gorgeous stately homes and gardens, or rummaging around in craft and antique shops. Almost inevitably, we would also end up spending a couple of hours in one of the country tea shops that are to be found in almost every village, no matter how small.

Two of my favourite villages were Chipping Campden, widely acknowledged to be one of the most beautiful in England, with its curving high street of honey-coloured buildings, and Bourton-on-the-Water, with little cottages lining the banks of the river that runs through the village.

Both of these villages possessed a number of tea shops, almost all equally charming, with flower-filled gardens in the summer, and roaring log fires in the winter. Tea was served in floral bone china cups and there were all sorts of good things to eat – cakes, of course, and

We do not remember days …
we remember moments.

CESARE PAVESE

scones, served with thick clotted cream and pots of strawberry preserves, and sometimes hot spicy teacakes, dripping with melted butter. It was a happy and treasured time in my life.

One of the nicest things about food memories is that we can recreate them in our kitchens anytime, and they are a wonderful way to remember special times shared with those we love. So I make tea and scones, haul out the pretty china, and celebrate with those who make every day a blessing!

Butterscotch Blondies

This is another typically American bar cookie, and personally it's one I prefer to the more common chocolate brownie – rather like a cross between fudge and a cookie. The chocolate chips can be any type you like – dark, milk or white chocolate. (I've also used butterscotch chips on occasion.) The macadamias are delicious, but pecans or walnuts are also good. A pan of these cookies makes a great gift for someone who is having a not-too-good day, or just to say 'hello'.

- 125 g butter
- 200 ml (160 g) brown sugar, packed
- 1 extra large egg
- 8 ml vanilla extract
- 125 ml (70 g) cake flour
- 5 ml baking powder
- 3 ml salt
- 125 ml (100 g) chocolate chips
- 125 ml (75 g) coarsely chopped macadamias or pecans

Preheat the oven to 180 °C. Grease a 20-cm square baking pan very well.

In a heavy saucepan, melt the butter over low heat, then remove from the heat and stir in the sugar until dissolved. Leave to cool for a few minutes, then add the egg and vanilla, and mix well.

In a bowl, sift together the flour, baking powder and salt, then add to the butter mixture and beat. Stir in the chocolate chips and nuts. Spread the batter evenly in the prepared pan and bake for 25–30 minutes, until the top is puffy and golden-brown; the inside of the blondies will still be a little soft, but should not be sticky or liquid. Leave to cool in the pan, then cut into squares. Store in the fridge in an airtight container.

Makes 16

There are four basic food groups: milk chocolate, dark chocolate, white chocolate and chocolate truffles.

AUTHOR UNKNOWN

Paradise Slices

Another one of those traditional cookie recipes – this one from Scotland, again – that never seems to really go out of style. I love the simplicity and honesty of recipes such as this, which evoke such a strong sense of continuity, both in the kitchen and in life.

BASE	TOPPING
90 g butter	2 eggs
80 ml (65 g) light brown sugar	250 ml (200 g) light brown sugar
310 ml (175 g) cake flour	80 ml (45 g) cake flour
1 egg yolk	5 ml baking powder
	3 ml salt
	125 ml (75 g) seedless raisins
	125 (75 g) seedless sultanas
	250 ml (80 g) desiccated coconut

Adapt what is useful, reject what is useless, and add what is specifically your own.

BRUCE LEE

Preheat the oven to 180 °C. Grease a 20 x 30 cm baking pan well, and line the base with baking paper.

Melt the butter and 80 ml sugar together over a gentle heat, then leave to cool briefly. Stir in the flour and egg yolk, and mix to form a soft dough. Press the dough evenly over the base of the prepared pan. Bake for about 10 minutes, or until very pale gold in colour. Leave to cool.

For the topping, beat the eggs and 250 ml sugar together well, until smooth and thick. Sift the flour, baking powder and salt together, then fold into the egg mixture. Stir in the raisins and sultanas, and then the coconut. Spread the topping over the cooled base, and return to the oven for another 25–30 minutes, until the topping is pale brown and set. Leave to cool in the pan before cutting into bars or squares.

Makes 20–24

Victorias

The name 'Victorias' is how these little chocolate tarts are known in France, or so I was told by my friend Tersia, a good boeremeisie *who went to France a few years ago, following her heart and an enigmatic Frenchman. That romance did not last, especially once she discovered he already had a wife, but a new love was born – for a country. These days she lives in a small village in Provence, among fields of lavender. Sadly, I have not yet had the opportunity to visit her there, but she sends me yummy recipes and enticing photographs. These chocolate tarts are one of the delights on offer at the local patisserie; obviously they will not divulge the recipe, but we have concocted our own. I used to make chocolate tarts with a baked filling, but now I think I prefer these ones filled with smooth and decadent chocolate ganache.*

PASTRY

500 ml (280 g) cake flour
60 ml (50 g) castor sugar
185 g chilled butter
1 egg
1 egg yolk

CHOCOLATE FILLING

250 g dark chocolate, chopped
125 ml (105 g) castor sugar
200 ml cream
1 egg yolk

GARNISH

whipped cream, grated nuts or chocolate pieces

First make the pastry, which has to rest in the fridge for at least 1 hour. In a large bowl, combine the flour and sugar, then rub in the chilled butter until the mixture resembles breadcrumbs. Stir in the egg and egg yolk, and mix to form a dough. (If the dough does not combine well, add 1–2 tablespoons of cream.) Shape the dough into a ball, cover with plastic wrap and chill in the fridge for 1 hour.

Preheat the oven to 180 °C.

On a floured board, roll out the dough thinly – no more than 4 mm thick. This makes enough for about 10 x 10-cm tartlets, or alternatively you can make smaller tarts in muffin or patty pans. Whatever size you choose, cut out a circle about 3 cm larger than the diameter of the pan you are using. Carefully, without stretching the dough, press it into the pan. Trim any edges that hang over the tops of the pans. Prick all over the bottom of each tart with a fork, then bake the pastry shells for 15–20 minutes, until they are golden-brown and firm. Use a spatula to place them on a wire rack and leave to cool completely before filling with the chocolate.

To make the filling (while the tarts are baking and cooling); combine the chocolate, sugar and cream in a glass bowl over a pan of simmering water. Stir until the chocolate has melted completely, and the sugar dissolved. Leave the mixture to cool slightly. Beat the egg yolk lightly with a fork, then stir into the chocolate mixture. Cover the filling, and chill for a short while; it will thicken.

Spoon a little chocolate filling into each tart shell, ensuring that none runs down the sides. Refrigerate for at least 3–4 hours, then remove from the fridge about 20 minutes before serving. Garnish as desired.

Makes ±4 large tarts or ±12 small tarts

The way is not in the sky. The way is in the heart.

GAUTAMA BUDDHA

Hello Dollys

An American man, with whom I once had a brief and bittersweet romance, was the one who told me about these, which he said his mother had often made for him when he was young. He could give me few details, apart from the fact that they contained condensed milk, nuts, biscuits and chocolate, and that they were irresistibly delicious! (As was he.) Later, I did my own research, and found that versions of this cookie/bar are really plentiful, with many people claiming to have the 'original' recipe. No matter, for I like this one just fine, and so does anyone I make it for, even while their hips (and dentists) are probably cursing me.

175 g digestive biscuits, crumbed
60 ml (50 g) light brown sugar
60 g unsalted butter
125 g pecan nuts, coarsely chopped
90 g dark or milk chocolate chips
125 ml (40 g) desiccated coconut
90 g butterscotch chips (optional)
397g can condensed milk

Preheat the oven to 160 °C. Grease a fairly deep, 23-cm square baking pan well or line it with aluminium foil.

Combine the biscuit crumbs and sugar in a bowl. Melt the butter, then pour over the crumb mixture and mix lightly (it will look like sand). Press evenly into the base of the prepared pan and bake for 10 minutes, until just starting to brown. Leave to cool for 10 minutes.

Stir together the nuts, chocolate chips, coconut and butterscotch chips (if using), then sprinkle this mixture evenly over the biscuit base. Pour all the condensed milk over the top, using a spatula to spread it evenly. Bake for 30–35 minutes until light golden on top. Leave to cool completely in the pan, then cover the pan, and refrigerate for at least 3–4 hours before cutting into squares. Eat as soon as possible (which is not a hardship!) as they tend to become soft and sticky.

Makes ±16

To miss the joy is to miss all ...

ROBERT LOUIS STEVENSON

Cookie Magic

A few years ago an American friend introduced me to the concept of cookie ('biscuit' to us in South Africa) exchanges at Christmas time; these are apparently a popular feature of the holidays in the US. Of course I grew up making lots of cookies and other sweet treats with my Mom to give as Christmas gifts, but the idea of a cookie exchange is somewhat different.

Basically, a group gets together and each person in the group brings a generous quantity of their favourite homemade cookies (biscuits). These are divided up among the guests, who then go home with a nice assortment of holiday goodies – after a bit of a festive party, of course! It's a great idea, but let's be honest, most of us probably don't need to eat too many biscuits.

However, the whole concept becomes even more meaningful if we know our handmade treats are going to sweeten someone else's life.

So, I ask family and friends to bring plenty of their favourite biscuits, as per the American tradition – plus a few extra for the guests to sample! Set out drinks – juice, tea, coffee, maybe a little festive punch, too. The creative part comes in the packaging of the biscuits. For this you will need to have a good supply of plain boxes and

brown paper bags, plus lots of different trimmings, such as stickers, ribbons and colourful tissue paper for lining the containers.

It's a lot of fun decorating the boxes and bags as beautifully as possible, then dividing the different biscuits between them. Some ideas for possible recipients include shelters for women and children, the homeless, retirement homes, places of safety for children, caring organisations such as the Salvation Army … everyone needs a little cookie magic, especially at Christmas time!

Christmas is not as much about opening our presents, as opening our hearts.

JANICE MAEDITERE

Swedish Holiday Biscuits

My mom and I always made lots of biscuits in the run-up to Christmas, both as gifts and simply to serve to guests. This is a recipe for what are known as 'Spritz' biscuits in Sweden – buttery, soft and highly delicious. My mom usually piped them out in various shapes using a biscuit press, but I am rather lazy, and tend to roll them simply into rings!

250 g softened butter
200 ml (170 g) castor sugar
2 egg yolks
5 ml almond essence
625 ml (350 g) cake flour
5 ml salt
icing sugar for dusting or melted chocolate for drizzling (optional)

Preheat the oven to 200 °C. Grease 2 large baking sheets very well.

In a large mixing bowl, cream the butter and sugar until light and fluffy. Beat in the egg yolks and almond essence. Add the flour and salt gradually, beating well, until a soft dough is formed. (Refrigerate the dough for 30 minutes if it is too soft to handle.) Break off small balls of dough, shape each into a thin sausage and then into a ring with a 5-cm diameter.

Place the rings on the prepared baking sheets, leaving a little space between each. Bake for 10 minutes or until just pale golden. Use a spatula to place the biscuits on a wire rack. Dust with icing sugar or drizzle with melted chocolate when quite cold, if you like. They keep well for a couple of weeks in an airtight container.

Makes 50–60

At Christmas all roads lead home.

MARJORIE HOLMES

Cenci alla Fiorentina

This recipe for deep-fried pastries comes from a very old Italian cookbook we had when I was growing up. From the time I was old enough to fry things on my own, I loved making them, either just as a snack, or to serve after an Italian meal, with coffee.

- 500 ml (280 g) cake flour
- 2 eggs plus 1 egg yolk
- 30 ml brandy, rum or sherry
- 30 ml icing sugar
- 5 ml salt
- sunflower oil for frying
- icing sugar or honey for sprinkling

Sift the flour into a bowl. Make a well in the centre and pour in the eggs (including the extra egg yolk), brandy, 30 ml icing sugar and salt. Mix with a spoon until a dough starts to form. Turn out onto a floured board and knead well, until the dough is shiny and smooth. Cover and refrigerate for 1 hour.

Pour the oil (6–7 cm deep) into a heavy-bottomed frying pan, then heat the oil. Roll out the dough very thinly and cut it into strips approximately 11 cm long and 1.5 cm wide. Tie the strips into loose knots and fry, 4 or 5 at a time, until crisp and golden-brown. Drain on paper towel, then pile onto a plate. Serve sprinkled with icing sugar or honey.

Makes ±40

MANGIA!

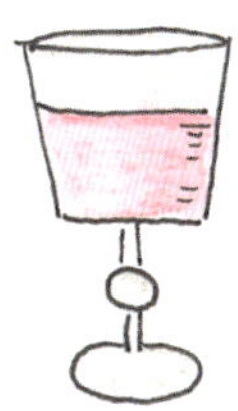

Believe in others. Believe in yourself. Believe in your dreams. If you don't, who will?

JON BON JOVI

Zuppa Inglese

The Italian name sounds very romantic. Less so is the English translation – 'English soup'. This is something Anna, the Italian mother of one of my school friends, used to make. In fact, I even think she made several of these for the party after our matric dance. It's a trifle, in a way, but it's also a really simple recipe, with no actual baking involved. And it does look rather spectacular, with the colourful layers showing through the sides of the glass dish.

225 g jar maraschino cherries
125 ml rum or brandy
500 ml whipping cream
375 ml vanilla custard
10 ml castor sugar
200 g packet Boudoir biscuits (lady fingers)
65 g slivered almonds
310 g can mandarin oranges, drained

Drain the cherries, but reserve the juice and mix it with the rum or brandy. Slice the cherries in half. Whip the cream, then fold half of it into the custard. Stir the sugar into the other half, and set aside.

Arrange a layer of biscuits in the bottom of a deep glass dish with straight sides. (If necessary, break the biscuits to fit.) Sprinkle with some of the cherry-rum liquid, then scatter a few of the sliced cherries on top. Spread a third of the custard-cream over them. Repeat this layering process twice more, ending with a final layer of biscuits and cherry-rum liquid. Spread the remaining whipped cream over the biscuits, and sprinkle with the almonds. Finally, decorate with the mandarin oranges. Refrigerate for at least 2 hours before serving, and then ... *mangia!*

Serves 10–12

The trouble with eating Italian food is that, five or six days later you're hungry again.

GEORGE MILLER

Banoffee Pie

On my travels through Britain, this delicious pudding – if that is the right word for it – turned up everywhere. It's really easy to put together, and unfortunately even easier to eat, given that it probably has 5 000 kilojoules in a slice! But sometimes one needs to forget about such things and simply enjoy the moment. (I like to use a large pizza pan to make this, which I line with aluminium foil first, but you can also use a large baking pan if you prefer).

- 185 g butter, melted
- 300 g digestive biscuits, finely crushed
- 4 large, ripe bananas
- 30 ml lemon juice
- 360 g can Nestlé caramel treat
- 375 ml cream

There are times to stay put, and what you want will come to you, and there are times to go out into the world and find such a thing for yourself.

LEMONY SNICKET

Preheat the oven to 180 °C. Line a pizza pan with baking paper or grease a baking pan very well.

Stir the butter into the biscuit crumbs. Press the mixture evenly over the base of the prepared pan, then bake for 10 minutes. Leave to cool.

Slice the bananas quite thinly, and sprinkle them with the lemon juice. Arrange the slices evenly over the cooled biscuit base. Spread the caramel treat over the bananas, covering them completely. Whip the cream until stiff, then spread it over the caramel layer. Chill for at least 30 minutes before serving – with more cream, if you dare!

Serves 6–8

Apple and Almond Galette

Quite honestly, a lot of apple pies are a bit boring, with thick pastry that shares its origin with cardboard. This one is not like that – at all. It's also relatively quick and easy, because you use ready-made puff pastry, which makes the whole thing a cinch! Galettes were first made in France, and are really versatile as they can be served for brunch, at teatime, or as a great dessert.

400 g pack frozen puff pastry, thawed
60 g softened butter
60 ml (50 g) castor sugar
5 ml almond extract
1 egg
125 ml (50 g) ground almonds
4 Granny Smith apples, peeled, cored and thinly sliced
30 ml granulated white sugar mixed with
5 ml ground cinnamon
icing sugar for dusting

Preheat the oven to 200 °C. Grease a large baking sheet very well.

Roll the pastry a little bit thinner than it is, and cut out a circle with a diameter of approximately 28 cm. (You will probably not need to use all the pastry.) Place it on the prepared baking sheet.

Cream together the butter, castor sugar and almond extract. Beat in the egg, followed by the ground almonds, to make a smooth paste. Spread the paste over the circle of pastry, leaving a margin of about 4 cm all round.

Arrange the apple slices evenly on top of the paste, then sprinkle with the granulated sugar and cinnamon mixture. Fold up the sides of the pastry, to create a rim around the apples. Bake for 30–35 minutes, until the pastry is golden-brown and the apples soft. Slide the galette onto a wire rack and leave to cool. Dust with icing sugar before serving. (It tastes good warm or cold.)

Serves 6–8

*I believe that tomorrow is another day
and I believe in miracles.*

AUDREY HEPBURN

LeMae's Arkansas Cornbread

LeMae told me there were probably as many different recipes for cornbread as there are cooks in the American South – and of course everyone thinks his or her cornbread is the best. This is a good basic recipe, which can be tweaked in a number of ways, by adding chopped cooked bacon, grated cheese or onion, for example. I have added the corn kernels and chillis because that's the way LeMae made hers, but you can leave them out if you prefer. (I did, however, reduce the amount of sugar, because I found her bread a little too sweet.) This cornbread may be served warm or cold, any time of the day; it's particularly good with soup or a casserole, and, of course, a wonderful side dish at a braai.

I think it pisses God off if you walk by the colour purple in a field somewhere, and don't notice it ...

ALICE WALKER

250 ml (120 g) yellow cornflour (fine) or fine polenta	2 eggs
250 ml (140 g) cake flour	375 ml buttermilk
15 ml baking powder	60 g butter, melted
5 ml salt	250 ml corn kernels (fresh or frozen)
30 ml granulated white sugar	15 ml chopped green chillis

Preheat the oven to 200 °C. Grease a fairly deep, 23-cm square baking pan very well.

In a large mixing bowl, combine the cornflour or polenta, cake flour, baking powder, salt and sugar. In another bowl, beat together the eggs, buttermilk and melted butter. Stir into the dry ingredients, then beat well to form a thick, smooth batter. Lastly, stir in the corn kernels and chillis. Spoon the batter evenly into the prepared pan, and bake for approximately 25 minutes, until the bread is risen and golden. Leave to cool briefly in the pan, then turn out onto a wire rack.

Cut into squares. It's best served as fresh as possible.

Makes 9 generous squares

Onion and Bacon Round Bread

Marie, a friend of mine from Belgium, sent me this recipe a few years ago; it actually comes from Alsace, in northern France, where it is served on its own as a snack, or with soups, salads and barbecues. Marie told me she often replaces the bacon with slivers of Parma ham or prosciutto, and sometimes I prefer this, as bacon can be a little fatty. The cream must be very thick; ordinary cream is not suitable. If you can't get really thick farm cream, use crème fraîche instead – it works beautifully.

BREAD

- 250 ml lukewarm milk
- 25 g cube fresh yeast (or 10 ml dried)
- 2 eggs
- 60 g butter, melted
- 1 litre (560 g) cake flour
- 5 ml salt

TOPPING

- 45 ml butter
- 2 small onions, thinly sliced
- 125 g streaky bacon, chopped
- 250 ml thick cream or crème fraîche
- salt and freshly ground black pepper to taste

*The very least you can do with your life is figure out what you hope for.
And the most you can do is live inside that hope.*

BARBARA KINGSOLVER

Grease a large, 30-cm pizza pan or a large (25 x 30 cm) rectangular baking pan very well.

For the bread, in a large bowl combine the milk and yeast, stirring until the yeast dissolves. Beat in the eggs, and then the butter. Sift the flour and salt together, then add to the yeast mixture, stirring well until it forms a soft dough. Turn onto a floured surface and knead for 5 minutes, until the dough is smooth and elastic.

Return to the bowl, cover with a clean cloth and leave to rise in a warm place for 1 hour, or until it has doubled in size.

To make the topping, melt the butter in a saucepan, and gently fry the onions and bacon together until the onion is soft and golden, and the bacon cooked. Remove from the heat and leave to cool completely before stirring in the cream or crème fraîche, and salt and pepper.

Preheat the oven to 200 °C. Knock down the risen dough, then press it evenly into the prepared pan; it should be about 1 cm thick. Leave it for about 15 minutes, to rise again. Use your fingertips to make small indentations across the surface of the risen dough, then spread with the topping. Bake for 20–25 minutes, until the bread is done and the topping is bubbling and golden. Cut into wedges or squares, and serve immediately, if possible.

Serves 10

Crustless Tomato, Cheese and Olive Tart

I have a number of friends who live in Australia and New Zealand, and one of them, Laura, put me onto the cookbooks written by Australian food writer, Belinda Jeffery. Her recipes are both delicious and accessible, and written in a charming style. This crustless tart was inspired by the wonderful Zucchini and Feta Pie, in her Mix and Bake *book, but I have given it something more of an Italian flavour, with olives and tomatoes. It makes such a nice, easy meal, served with a big salad and lots of chilled white wine!*

375 ml (210 g) cake flour
10 ml baking powder
60 ml grated Parmesan cheese
125 g crumbled feta cheese
125 ml (50 g) grated Cheddar cheese
125 g butter

3 eggs
60 ml milk
60 ml chopped fresh oregano
a handful stoned olives, chopped
10 cherry tomatoes, halved
extra grated Parmesan cheese (optional)

Preheat the oven to 180 °C. Grease a round or square 25-cm baking pan very well.

In a large mixing bowl, combine the flour, baking powder, Parmesan, feta and Cheddar. Melt the butter gently, leave to cool slightly, then beat together with the eggs and milk. Mix into the flour mixture, to make a fairly stiff batter. Mix in the oregano, and chopped olives. Spoon the batter into the prepared pan and arrange the cherry tomatoes evenly over the top. Sprinkle with additional Parmesan, if you like.

Bake for 35–40 minutes, or until the tart has risen and is golden-brown. Leave to cool before removing from the pan. This tart may be served either warm or cold.

Serves 6

Bacon and Onion Pots

It's funny how things served individually, as little pies or whatever, always look nicer than one large item. I remember eating a version of these at a little tea shop on the south coast of England on a particularly cold and blustery winter day; they were so warming, with a simple, honest flavour. When I decided to recreate them, I used my mom's old cheese pastry recipe, though, as it is crisp and full of flavour.

PASTRY
250 ml (140 g) cake flour
250 ml (100 g) grated Cheddar cheese
salt and pepper to taste
125 g cold butter, cubed

FILLING
2 small onions, finely chopped
125 g streaky bacon, chopped
butter for frying
2 eggs
250 ml cream
30 ml cake flour
freshly ground black pepper
15 ml Parmesan cheese
15 ml chopped fresh parsley

Faith is taking the first step, even when you can't see the whole staircase.

MARTIN LUTHER KING

Preheat the oven to 180 °C. Grease about 10 regular muffin pan cups very well.

For the pastry, combine the flour and cheese in a bowl, with salt and pepper to taste. Using your fingertips, rub in the cold butter until the mixture resembles coarse breadcrumbs, then mix to form a dough (you may need a few spoons of cold water as well). Shape the dough into balls and press each into a muffin pan cup as evenly as possible, over the base and up the sides. Prick the bases with a fork, and bake for 10 minutes, until just starting to go golden.

For the filling, fry the onions and bacon together in a little butter until the onions are soft and the bacon cooked. Drain and leave to cool completely. Beat together the eggs, cream and remaining ingredients well. Sprinkle the onion and bacon mixture evenly over the base of each small pastry pot. Pour the egg mixture over this, also as evenly as possible. Bake for 25–30 minutes, or until the filling is set and golden-brown. These are best served warm.

Makes ±10

Zwiebelewahe (Swiss Cheese and Onion Tart)

My first 'proper' job was as a junior typist for a firm of architects. Quite frankly, it was very boring, but one bonus was, because it was quite a small business, everyone in the office took turns to bring treats for tea or lunch, on a daily basis. For a while a Swiss woman worked with us, and she brought the most delicious cheese and onion tart, which she said was a speciality of Zurich. I loved it, but never had the recipe until a few years ago, when someone gave me a beautiful book by Manuela Darling-Ganssen called Winter in the Alps. *It's a stunning book, part travel and part cookery, and in it is the recipe for this tart – just as I remembered it. I have changed it a little, reducing the onions, and using a different cheese, but thank you, Manuela, for the original!*

8 ml dry yeast (not instant)
125 ml warm water
5 ml granulated white sugar
500 ml (280 g) cake flour
5 ml salt
125 g butter

FILLING
125 g streaky bacon, chopped
30 ml olive oil
60 g butter
3 onions, peeled and thinly sliced
4 eggs
250 ml cream
250 ml (100 g) grated Cheddar cheese
salt and pepper to taste

For the pastry crust, combine the yeast, water and sugar in a small bowl, then set aside until the sugar and yeast have dissolved (about 10 minutes). In another bowl, mix the flour and salt, then rub in the butter. Pour in the yeast mixture and mix well to form a smooth and shiny dough (add a little water if it seems too dry). Leave the pastry dough to rise for about 30 minutes (it won't rise a lot).

Preheat the oven to 220 °C. Grease a round, 25-cm pie dish well.

Fry the bacon in the oil until crisp, but not hard. Drain and leave to cool on paper towel, then set aside. In the same pan, melt the butter and fry the onions until they are soft and golden. Drain then mix with the bacon. Press the pastry over the base and sides of the prepared dish. Scatter the onion-bacon mixture over the pastry base. Beat the eggs and cream together well, then stir in the cheese and salt and pepper. Pour into the pastry base, then bake for about 30 minutes, or until the filling is set and golden-brown. Serve warm.

Serves 4–6

Anything is possible. Anything can be.

SHEL SILVERSTEIN

Index

Conversion chart

METRIC TO IMPERIAL	
Teaspoons	
Metric	Imperial
2 ml	¼ tsp
3 ml	½ tsp
5 ml	1 tsp
10 ml	2 tsp
20 ml	4 tsp
Tablespoons	
Metric	Imperial
15 ml	1 Tbsp
30 ml	2 Tbsp
45 ml	3 Tbsp
60 ml	4 Tbsp
Cups	
Metric	Imperial
60 ml	¼ cup
80 ml	⅓ cup
125 ml	½ cup
160 ml	⅔ cup
200 ml	¾ cup
250 ml	1 cup
375 ml	1½ cups
500 ml	2 cups
750 ml	3 cups
1 litre	4 cups
Weights	
Metric	Imperial
30 g	1 oz
60 g	2 oz
125 g	4 oz
250 g	8 oz (½ lb)
500 g	16 oz (1 lb)
1 kg	2 lbs
2 kg	4 lbs
2.5 kg	5 lbs
Liquid	
Metric	Imperial
600 ml	1 pint
1.25 litres	2 pints
1.9 litres	3 pints
2.5 litres	4 pints

ESSENTIAL INGREDIENTS					
Ingredient	**¼ cup = 60 ml**	**⅓ cup = 80 ml**	**½ cup = 125 ml**	**¾ cup = 200 ml**	**1 cup = 250 ml**
Flour: cake, self-raising, white or brown bread, nutty wheat	35 g	45 g	70 g	110 g	140 g
Sugar: castor	50 g	70 g	105 g	170 g	210 g
Sugar: granulated (white or brown)	50 g	65 g	100 g	160 g	200 g
Sugar: icing	35 g	45 g	65 g	100 g	130 g
BASIC INGREDIENTS					
Butter			115 g		230 g
Coconut, desiccated	20 g	25 g	40 g	65 g	80 g
Raisins, sultanas	40 g	50 g	75 g	120 g	150 g

OTHER INGREDIENTS	
Ingredient	**Gram per 1 cup = 250 ml**
Biscuit crumbs	120 g
Breadcrumbs, dried	120 g
Breadcrumbs, fresh	60 g
Cheese, Cheddar or Gouda, grated	100 g
Cheese, mozzarella, grated	125 g
Chocolate chips	200 g
Cornflour	120 g
Dates	150 g
Nuts, almonds, grated	100 g
Nuts, almonds, chopped or slivered	150 g
Nuts, chopped	150 g
Nuts, whole	100 g
Oats, rolled	80 g